DEPARTMENT OF THE ENVIRONMENT
SCOTTISH OFFICE
WELSH OFFICE

The Repair and Compensation System for Coal Mining Subsidence Damage

REPORT OF THE SUBSIDENCE COMPENSATION REVIEW COMMITTEE

LONDON: HER MAJESTY'S STATIONERY OFFICE

The Rt Hon Peter Walker MBE MP
Secretary of State for Energy

The Rt Hon Patrick Jenkin MP
Secretary of State for the Environment

The Rt Hon George Younger MP
Secretary of State for Scotland

The Rt Hon Nicholas Edwards MP
Secretary of State for Wales

Sirs

We were appointed in February 1983 to examine the practical problems of the operation of the repair and compensation system for coal mining subsidence damage and to consider possible improvements.

We now have pleasure in submitting our Report.

Lewis E Waddilove (*Chairman*)

Michael A Baatz

Jean Horsham

Eric King

David G McKinlay

Peter Vincent

Tom V Walters

Anita Woolman

16 March 1984

MEMBERS OF THE SUBSIDENCE COMPENSATION REVIEW COMMITTEE AND THEIR TECHNICAL ASSESSORS

Chairman

Lewis E Waddilove Esq
CBE JP

Former Director, Joseph Rowntree Memorial Trust

Former Deputy Chairman, Housing Corporation

Chairman, University of York Council

Chairman, Central Appeals Advisory Committee

Members

Michael A Baatz Esq
MA FRSA

Retired Registrar, Secretary and Finance Officer, University of Leicester

Member, National Insurance Local Tribunal

Member, Leicester Housing Association

Miss Jean Horsham CBE

Retired Deputy Parliamentary Commissioner for Administration

Eric King Esq BSc CEng FICE

Retired Project Manager, ESSO Petroleum (UK)

Professor David G McKinlay BSc PhD CEng FICE

Professor of Civil Engineering, University of Strathclyde

Member of Council, Institution of Civil Engineers

Peter A Vincent Esq FRICS
CEng MIMinE FIQ

Partner, Smith, Vincent & Co Chartered Mineral Surveyors and Consulting Mining Engineers

Tom V Walters Esq CBE DL

A Solicitor

Former County Clerk and Chief Executive of Mid Glamorgan County Council, and Clerk of the South Wales Police Authority

Former Chairman, Association of County Chief Executives

Former Honorary Secretary, Welsh Counties Committee and adviser to various other public bodies in Wales

Mrs Anita Woolman JP

Member, Transport Users Consultative Committee (Yorkshire Area)

Magistrates Association (West Yorkshire), Leeds Bench Representative

Former Leeds City Councillor

Former Member, Leeds Eastern Community Health Council

Technical Assessors

Alan Dickie Esq FRICS CEng MICE

Director of Estates, National Coal Board

Peter Spurrier Esq CEng FRICS FIMinE

Chief Mining Engineer, South Yorkshire County Council

CONTENTS

ACKNOWLEDGEMENTS

CHAPTER 1

INTRODUCTION

1. We were appointed in February 1983 with the following terms of reference:

> "to examine the practical problems of the operation of the repair and compensation system for coal mining subsidence damage; to consider possible improvements; and to report".

These terms of reference were elaborated in a letter from John Moore MP, the then Parliamentary Under-Secretary of State for Energy, to our Chairman which included the following paragraph:

> "We need to know how far in practice, and in the considered opinion of the Committee, the present compensation system meets the real identifiable problems of people who suffer the effects of coal mining subsidence and whether there are significant areas of real grievance or hardship which it does not cover and for which it would be reasonable and practicable to make compensation provision. We are conscious of the danger that extending rights of compensation in the absence of clear evidence of need might result only in additional financial burdens on the National Coal Board and perhaps knock-on effects in other areas. We would like the Committee to examine the problems of subsidence damage compensation in this light, and to report. A specific question of this sort upon which we would be grateful for recommendations is that of residual loss of property values".

The Committee met for the first time on 29 March 1983 to consider the task implied by these terms of reference and to agree their approach to the work.

2. By way of introduction, we explain the lay-out and content of our report, and then give an account of the methods used to obtain the information on which we have based our conclusions. Before doing so, it is important to make clear how we have interpreted our terms of reference, and what has become the philosophical background to all our discussions and conclusions as our knowledge of our subject increased. An understanding of our corporate position as a Committee in relation to these matters is essential to a proper understanding of our report.

Terms of Reference and the Committee's Approach
3. The emphasis in our terms of reference, and in the Minister's letter, is on the effectiveness of the subsidence damage compensation scheme in meeting the problems of people affected by subsidence damage, and on identifying any gaps in the provisions to meet loss, disturbance and damage giving genuine grounds for complaint. Early in our work it became evident that claims for compensation had increased considerably in the last few years, and

1

there was a more than proportionate increase in those arising within the category of very severe damage. Some of that damage is so disruptive to the lives of families and individuals, often over a period of years, that it seemed to us that no "compensation" in the generally accepted meaning of that word was in fact possible. We concluded that our task must therefore include an examination of the reasons for this increased scale of damage, and how far it could be avoided or prevented. We have therefore taken a broad view of our terms of reference in considering the issues raised in evidence.

4. The enquiries, visits and discussions which we have initiated, and which are described later in this chapter, have led to some reflection on the future production and use of coal, and the wider energy scene. In 1962, coal contributed just over two thirds of Britain's primary energy supply: by 1982 that proportion had declined to rather more than a third. This was primarily due to the increased use of oil, natural gas and other energy sources, including nuclear power. Projections to the end of the century indicate that such a decline has almost certainly ceased and may even be reversed, although coal seems unlikely to regain its former dominant position amongst domestic sources of energy supply. Domestic coal production in 1982/83 was 120.9 million tonnes, whilst the Department of Energy's latest projections span a range of demand of 100–140 m.t.p.a. by the year 2000. Total capital investment by the board since 1974 has been over £4½ billion, and continues at about £800 million p.a. Coal is therefore expected to continue to play a major role in supplying our future energy needs but as one of a number of possible sources rather than as almost the sole source.

5. It precise role is expected to be influenced by developments in energy management, conservation and storage, by reaction to fears of resource depletion, and by changes in the use made of coal. Coal may, for example, be capable of conversion economically to liquid and gaseous fuels at the time when the predicted decline in oil and gas reserves begins to be felt. It is also – along with other fossil fuels – already a significant source of chemical feedstock, and this market can be expected to increase over future years. At the same time, concern for the short and long term environmental effects of coal production and use, particularly colliery spoil disposal and power station emissions to the atmosphere, is expected to grow. Tighter environmental controls on these and other aspects of the industry could affect the relative attractiveness of coal as a source of energy and as a raw material.

6. We mention these possible developments to illustrate the uncertain context within which the coal industry must operate, and the range of factors against which individual investment projects now need to be appraised. Damage from surface subsidence, and the subsequent cost of restitution, is but one such factor. It is however of growing public concern, and we think it right that in all future mining proposals a critical assessment of whether the need for coal outweighs the expected subsidence damage to people and property should form an important part any appraisal.

Framework of the Report
7. The evolution of the compensation system, the statutory and voluntary codes in which it is at present expressed, and the recent proposals for their

2

revision which have culminated in our appointment as a review committee, are discussed in Chapter 2. Chapter 3 covers the compensation system in practice as revealed by the evidence we received. We also look briefly at compensation provision in other fields of public and industrial development, and at comparable experience overseas. The chapter concludes by identifying the issues which emerge from the analysis and which are the subject of the remaining chapters in the report. In the following paragraphs we note the principles which inform our consideration of those issues.

8.   First, it cannot be right that surface damage should enter into the consideration of a proposed mining operation only as an item of monetary cost. The expected gains must be set against the human and physical damage that will result; this is very different from restoring buildings to a usable condition or demolishing and replacing those that are beyond repair. When as a result of a natural disaster or unpredictable catastrophe the continuity of home, family and community life is broken, it becomes a first claim on the social and other public services to restore it and to prevent a recurrence. We see no reason why similar responsibilities should not be accepted in respect of the more severe types of damage resulting from mining subsidence. If the cost of reducing surface damage to acceptable levels means that mining does not satisfy the Board's investment criteria, then this must be a factor in deciding whether the coal should be extracted at all. In Chapter 4 we apply these principles to decisions about the extension of mining operations and to the action that should be taken if severe damage is found to be both justifiable and unavoidable.

9.   Secondly, mining operations which are certain to cause disruption to homes and families, as well as to public and commercial interests, should not be initiated without any prior warning to those who may be the sufferers. We examine the matter of notification of mining operations and make recommendations about future practice in Chapter 5.

10.   Thirdly, we have found reason to question whether present arrangements for subsidence damage compensation take sufficient account of the significance of the "home" as the focus of family and personal life. For the rising proportion of the population who are owner-occupiers, the home is the largest capital asset the individual or family will ever own. For all, whether owners or tenants, a dwelling – with the accumulated furniture, fittings and adaptations chosen and often carried out by the occupants – expresses their individuality in a way not otherwise open to many in the increasingly impersonal world of work and community affairs. The problems presented by subsidence damage for the owners or occupiers of a dwelling are therefore of a different order from those experienced by corporate bodies in the private or public sector, however important their services to the community may be. Owners and tenants may face other losses consequent on the damage to their home; they wish to feel in control of what is happening to their home and possessions even though the cost of repair may rightly fall upon others; owner-occupiers may see a fall in the value of their property beyond any ordinary movement in the market. We consider these more personal aspects of subsidence damage in Chapters 6 and 7.

11.   Fourthly, it is not acceptable that a public body which causes damage to homes and property should appear to be the sole judge of the extent of its liability for damage to a particular property, and the amount and kind of compensation that should be paid. The demand for some immediate and accessible independent adjudication [1] in disputes in these matters has been expressed by almost all who have given evidence to us, whether individuals or corporate bodies. We make proposals for new provisions for this purpose in Chapter 8.

12.   Fifthly, the legislative, discretionary and administrative provision dealing with subsidence damage have become very complicated and confusing; rights and choices which may be clear to those who operate the system often elude the householder seeking help and, not infrequently, even some who offer professional advice. We make proposals in Chapters 5 and 9 to make technical and other information more easily available, and in Chapter 9 we indicate the shape of a simpler and more comprehensive statutory code.

Collection of Evidence and the Independent Survey

13.   We turn now to the methods we have used to obtain the information on which our conclusions and recommendations have been based. With the help of our Technical Assessors and officers of the National Coal Board, we first gained some familiarity with the technical aspects of mining subsidence, and then gave priority in the use of our time over three months to visiting areas affected by mining subsidence, meeting in their homes families who had suffered damage and talking to private individuals who had written to us. We are indebted to local newspapers in mining areas, and to local radio stations, for giving wide and effective publicity to our wish to hear from and meet householders whose homes had suffered damage, and who had experience of negotiations with the Board on compensation. Several local authorities made meeting rooms available, provided a reception service for our visitors, and offered them refreshment in what many of them clearly feared might be a trying experience. In all, four hundred and twenty eight householders sent us letters about their experience; all were acknowledged and seventy two came by invitation to a convenient centre and replied helpfully to our enquiries at informal sessions of between thirty and fifty minutes. On other visits, officials of the Board took us to housing areas in which damage had occurred; we indicated a house at random; the official called and explained our mission and asked if we could be received. He then withdrew. Almost invariably we were invited in and retain pleasant memories of vigorous discussions and invaluable opportunities to discern the human as well as the physical impact of a sometimes tragic experience. Many paid tribute to the helpfulness and concern shown by the representatives of the Board who dealt with their claims for compensation.

14.   Our visits included the principal mining areas of England, Scotland and Wales, and are listed in Annex D. For these discussions and visits, we worked in groups of two or three, accompanied by a member from our secretariat.

---

[1] We use the term 'adjudication' in preference to 'arbitration' so as to avoid confusion with settlements made under the Arbitration Acts.

Clearly our opportunity to check or verify the statements of these individual witnesses was limited. For the most part we were convinced of their integrity. But we resolved to make no attempt to investigate or pronounce judgement upon individual cases; specfic requests for help or advice were referred to the appropriate authorities. Our purpose was to understand how subsidence damage and the compensation system appeared to those immediately affected and we believe that this purpose was achieved.

15.   Apart from public invitations to submit evidence, we wrote to sixty nine representatives bodies and individuals asking if they wished to provide written evidence. These included local authority associations, professional bodies, statutory undertakings and similar corporated bodies providing public services, residents' associations and agents offering advice on subsidence compensation. We also wrote to Members of Parliament for mining constituencies. We have also had consultations with the National Coal Board at Headquarters and in the Areas, and invited the views of the mining unions. We sought advice on particular questions from the Lands Tribunal and the Council on Tribunals, and from university departments committed to teaching and research in fields relevant to our work. A list of those who responded is given in Annex F. Of these, thirty eight accepted an invitation to meet members of the Committee in discussion; these are identified by an asterisk in the same Annex. These discussions took place in September and October 1983 at the end of our journeyings; usually cach discussion occupied up to two hours. We record our appreciation of the care with which all these submissions were prepared, and for the time given by so many in travelling to London for sessions which, with few exceptions, included all the members of our Committee.

16.   We were told at the outset by the Department of Energy that we might commission an independent survey of householders who had been affected by mining subsidence. We decided to do this in order to put in perspective the direct reprcsentations made to us on our visits and in the letters we received. We were very conscious that those who wrote to us were likely to be those most dissatisfied with their experience of the present compensation system. The survey was designed to provide an independent assessment of the aspects of the subsidence repair and compensation system that cause concern to individuals; to explore the scale and nature of the 'take-up' problem; and to identify points of view and problems that are important to members of the public who actually suffer from the effects of mining subsidence. Analysis of the survey results enabled us to confirm or modify the views we had formed from the direct evidence gathered from our visits and discussions. Full details of the survey are given in Annex G.

17.   The account that we have given of our sources of information will, we hope, show that we have cast our net wide. We have been greatly helped throughout our work by the Technical Assessors assigned to us by the National Coal Board and by the local authority associations. A more adequate tribute to their work appears at the end of our report together with other acknowledgements, but we feel it right to include them in this short review of the sources of information and advice which have made our work possible.

CHAPTER 2

BACKGROUND TO THE PRESENT COMPENSATION SYSTEM

We describe in this chapter the main provisions of subsidence legislation, and include a brief commentary on the developments leading up to the establishment of our Committee.

18.   The statutory and non-statutory provisions that make up the present subsidence compensation system are not straightforward. They are the product of a long and often tangled legal history, reflecting the balance struck at the time between the rights of surface owners and those of the owners of the coal and other minerals beneath the land surface. This chapter describes how the system has evolved, highlighting the particular provisions which are important to an understanding of current practice.

Common Law Rights and Severance of Interests
19.   At common law a surface owner had an absolute right of support for the surface of his land, that is a right to have the surface kept at its ancient and natural level. When the freehold in the underlying mineral deposits, such as coal, was severed from surface interests, or where mining leases were granted, the right to let down the surface of the land was also normally negotiated by the mining concern and the agreements made sometimes contained provision for compensation for certain surface damage resulting from mining subsidence. These provisions continue to run with the land for the benefit of the surface owner. As a result of these agreements many areas of land were deprived of any legal right to compensation for mining damage, and subsequent legislation has, in part, re-instated those rights which had previously been bargained away.

Mining Code
20.   Whilst the right to support could be abrogated in this way, it was felt important to protect certain installations from subsidence for safety reasons. Consequently a series of Acts was passed (beginning with the Railway Clauses Consolidation Act 1845), from which a set of rules was derived known as the Mining Code. This gave certain public utilities such as the railway companies the right to prevent the working of coal under their land or installations, although a compensation payment was then due to the mineral owner for the "sterilised" coal. These provisions still apply to certain public undertakings and to some local authority land, but since they concern the purchase of rights of support rather than compensation for subsidence damage we have not considered them further.

Coal Act 1938
21.   One of the most important changes in the law relating to support was brought about by the Coal Act 1938. This Act set up the Coal Commission in which was vested the ownership of virtually all the coal in the country. Where ownership of the coal was separate from that of the surface above it and there

6

was a right to let down the surface, this right passed to the Commission but with liability for subsidence compensation only where there was an existing right to compensation derived from a previous mining lease or from a conveyance or lease of the surface. Where the surface and the coal were still in the same ownership, the coal passed to the Commission, together with a right to let down the surface, subject to the requirement either to pay "proper compensation" or to make good any damage. For the first time, except in those cases where the title expressly provided otherwise, a general right to work coal was granted in return for a general liability for compensation for subsidence damage.

22. In certain cases, the 1938 Act also gave the Commission the right to make proposals regarding the specifications for foundations for new buildings, so as to minimise possible damage from future subsidence. The Commission had to bear any additional expense of incorporating its proposals, but, if they were not adopted, the Commission were no longer liable for any damage that would have been prevented.

Nationalisation and the Turner Report on Subsidence Compensation

23. On 1 January 1947 all the rights and liabilities of the Coal Commission, including those relating to subsidence, were transferred to the National Coal Board, created by the Coal Industry Nationalisation Act 1946. At the same time the Minister of Fuel and Power appointed the Turner Committee "to examine the law of support and the problem of damage caused by mining subsidence in the light of the nationalisation of coal and the coal mining industry, and to make recommendations."

24. Their report, presented to Parliament in March 1949 (Cmd 7637), noted the wide variety of compensation provisions then in force under both mining leases and statutory enactments. In their view this created an "illogical and chaotic state of the law" and often gave rise to unnecessary hardship and a real sense of grievance. The Committee therefore recommended a new and comprehensive scheme of compensation in substitution for existing rights which would provide for those surface owners without compensation rights under mining leases and who were not, therefore, covered by the 1938 Act.

Coal Mining (Subsidence) Act 1950

25. The Coal Mining (Subsidence) Act 1950 introduced more limited changes than those envisaged by the Turner Committee although it gave a general right of compensation or repair to owners of small dwelling houses, including those who had no rights under title. Amongst its other provisions were time limits for notice of damage, and the right for the Board to serve notice to the effect that permanent repair or compensation payments might be deferred until the likelihood of further subsidence damage had passed. Provision for this type of notice (known generally as a "stop notice", the term we use in this report) recurs in later legislation. The Act was repealed in 1973.

Coal Mining (Subsidence) Act 1957

26. The next legislative development, the 1957 Act, remains one of the cornerstones of the current compensation system. Most importantly it

extended statutory rights of compensation to owners of virtually all land, buildings and works damaged or otherwise affected by subsidence, apart from a few rare exceptions covered by Working Facilities Orders (see para 36) or where the interested parties agree to contract out from compensation under the Act. The Act specifically applies to any subsidence damage occuring since it became law. But as such damage may result from workings prior to the Act, claims relating to the recent collapse of old shallow coal workings can therefore still be made against the Board as long as the damage itself does not pre-date the Act.

27.   The Act requires the Board to carry out such works as to make the damaged property "reasonably fit" for its normal use. Alternatively the Board may elect to make a payment equal to the cost reasonably incurred by any other person in executing remedial works or, where the work will be merged with other work or redevelopment, to make payments equivalent to that which the Board would have had to spend on the subsidence damage alone. The Board may also elect, in certain circumstances, to make a payment to the claimant equal to the depreciation in the value of the property caused by the subsidence damage if the cost of remedial works would exceed that amount.

28.   Section 2(1) of the 1957 Act makes provision for a time limit, from the date when damage was first apparent, within which the claimant must give the Board written notice of subsidence damage. The particulars required in the notice (known as a "damage notice"), and a time limit of two months subject to extension for reasonable delay on appeal to the Board or the Secretary of State for Energy, are prescribed by Regulations made under the Act (SI 1957/1405). Section 3 of the Act also contains provisions, similar to those under the 1950 Act, for the deferment of repairs or compensation if it appears possible that further subsidence will occur. If owners or occupiers believe their dwelling to be uninhabitable through mining subsidence damage they may serve a Notice of Uninhabitability on the Board under Schedule 1 of the Act and as prescribed under the Regulations (SI 1957/1404). The Board, if in agreement, must then make available suitable alternative accommodation for the full period of dispossession.

29.   Section 4 of the Act allows the Board to carry out, with the consent of the owner, preventive works such as trenching around a building, which can reduce the damage caused by future subsidence. If owners of the property in question unreasonably withhold their consent to these works the Board are no longer liable for the damage that would have been prevented.

30.   With respect to land drainage, Section 5 of the Act includes a special provision requiring the Board to carry out measures, agreed with the appropriate drainage authority where possible, for remedying, mitigating or preventing any deterioration in the drainage system through mining subsidence. Provisions governing the procedures to be followed by the Board and by the drainage authority to implement this section of the Act, and for the determination of questions arising between the two parties, are set out in Regulations (SI 1958/1486).

31.   Another important section of the Act concerns the determination of disputes. Section 13 provides for reference of disputes between the Board and the claimant in England and Wales to the County Court (for property with a net annual value not exceeding £100 or where all parties agree) or to the Lands Tribunal. Disputes relating to property in Scotland may be referred to the Sheriff. If, in any proceedings under the Act, the question arises whether any damage to property is coal mining subsidence damage, and the circumstances are such as to indicate that damage may be from mining subsidence, Section 13(1) places the onus of proof on the Board to show that the damage is not mining subsidence damage.

Coal Industry Act 1975

32.   The other main Act on which the current compensation system is based is the Coal Industry Act 1975. This Act extended and clarified the Board's rights to withdraw support in certain circumstances and reintroduced compensation provisions similar to those in the 1938 Act which it superseded. These provisions require the Board either to pay "proper compensation" for the subsidence damage or, with the consent of the claimant (which shall not be unreasonably withheld), to make good the damage to his reasonable satisfaction.

33.   Section 2 of the Act requires the Board, in those few locations where they did not previously have a right to mine coal, to give three months notice of their intention to withdraw support. The notice must indicate the land to which it relates and be published for two successive weeks in suitable newpapers circulating in the area to be mined, as well as in the London Gazette or, for land in Scotland, the Edinburgh Gazette. A copy of the notice must also be served on every planning authority covering the land to which the notice relates; and a copy or copies must be posted in conspicuous locations on the land itself.

34.   Where the Board previously had a right to mine coal, for the most part in the traditional mining areas, these notices under Section 2(5) are deemed to have been given, so making the 1975 Act generally applicable apart from a few exceptional cases; these include land in respect of which orders have been made under the Mines (Working Facilities and Support) Act, or land covered by special agreements.

35.   The 1975 Act, unlike the 1957 Act, has no provision concerning the onus of proof of liability for any damage, so that where liability is in dispute, the onus of proof lies with the claimant. However, for damage resulting from the withdrawal of support after the enactment of the 1975 Act a claim may generally be made under either the 1957 or the 1975 Act. Under Section 6 of the 1957 Act if the claim is unsuccessful, or withdrawn before it is determined, a new claim may be made under the other Act (or title deeds if relevant), but claims cannot be made simultaneously on the basis of more than one right. The 1975 Act also provides a right of appeal for the Lands Tribunal for Scotland to determine disputes there.

Working Facilities Orders

36.   In those circumstances where the Board do not have or are unable to negotiate rights to mine coal, the Board can apply under the Mines (Working Facilities and Support) Act 1966 for orders granting the Board the necessary facilities to work the coal. Application is now made to the Secretary of State for Trade and Industry, and thence to the High Court which may impose whatever compensation terms and conditions it thinks fit. Conversely, the owner of the surface interest may apply for an Order preventing the mining of coal on the grounds that it is more in the national interest that the coal should remain than that the surface should be damaged. Such cases are unusual, although there are some areas covered by such Orders.

The Code of Practice

37.   Despite these statutory provisions, pressure for improvements and extensions to the compensation system continued. In response, and following a review by a Government working party, the Board introduced a voluntary Code of Practice in 1976. The Code [1] originally set out five types of claim for which compensation could be given in addition to that available under legislation:

(i)   damage to chattels, for example, household effects, plant and machinery, livestock;

(ii)   home loss payments, where as a result of subsidence a person is permanently displaced from a dwelling;

(iii)   depreciation of crops, where, for example, disturbance of the land drainage system has caused a reduced crop yield;

(iv)   farm loss payments, where the subsidence damage is so severe that the farm cannot be worked profitably and the farmer moves to another farm;

(v)   additional compensation for tenant farmers where compensation for permanent damage to the land has been paid to the landowner.

The intention was that these should be drafted in specific terms so that they could be incorporated in statute at the appropriate time. The Code allows a dispute between the Board and the claimant on any of these items to be referred to independent arbitration.

38.   In addition, the Board have undertaken to relieve hardship caused by subsidence damage by dealing sympathetically with all claims and making special discretionary payments in certain circumstances. For example, where the owner of a house damaged by mining subsidence cannot sell the property at its undamaged value, the Board will, under certain conditions, consider buying the house at its undamaged value or making up the difference between the undamaged value and the actual sale price. The Board may also make payments for other costs incurred and arising directly from the subsidence

---

[1] Contained in the NCB publication "Compensation for Mining Subsidence Damage" (known as the "Brown Booklet").

claim, such as loss of pay for time off work and expenditure on cleaning up after repair.

39.   In 1978 the Board introduced as a supplement to the Code of Practice a system of contributions[2] towards the fees of a professional adviser, such as a surveyor, engaged by the claimant to help prepare and present his claim. This was prepared in consultation with the Royal Institution of Chartered Surveyors. No contribution is made, however, where the cost of repairs together with any monetary payment is less than £250. The Board may also, at their discretion, give a contribution in respect of legal fees.

Other Legislative Proposals

40.   Pressure to amend the legislative provisions for compensation has come in the form of two recent Private Member's Bills, from Jack Ashley CH MP in 1979 and from John Heddle MP in 1981. Mr. Ashley's Bill sought payment for loss of property value due to subsidence, compensation for loss of earnings when pursuing a claim and for stress and inconvenience while repairs were being carried out. It also proposed that an independent commission be established to decide on the Board's liability and to administer the scheme. Mr. Heddle's Bill similarly sought compensation for consequential loss and the establishment of new mining subsidence tribunals to determine disputes in all but very large claims (above £10,000). It would have required wider, individual notice of withdrawal of support and the registration as a local land charge of any notification by the Board to a local planning authority that an area was one of past, present or future coal working. Neither Bill succeeded in reaching the statute book.

Commission on Energy and the Environment and the Government's White Paper

41.   In 1981 the Commission on Energy and the Environment published their first major report, on coal and the environment [3]. They concluded that there were no insuperable environmental obstacles to the role of coal as then envisaged, subject to important qualifications concerning spoil disposal, opencast extraction and subsidence. On subsidence, the Commission emphasised the need for repair work to be carried out speedily, efficiently and sensitively, and recommended the addition of a right to compensation for any residual loss of property value following the completion of repairs. Other recommendations covered further research into subsidence prediction, the incorporation of precautionary measures into planning conditions, and additional notification.

42.   In a White Paper in response to the Commission's report[4] the Government announced agreement with the Board on a number of measures designed to improve the lot of those affected by subsidence damage. These included a new form of notice to be published annually, and an updated

---

[2] Contained in the NCB publication "Supplement on Claimant's Surveyors Fees" (known as the "Green Leaflet").
[3] Commission on Energy and the Environment, 'Coal and the Environment' HMSO 1981
[4] 'Coal and the Environment' Cmnd 8877. May 1983

explanatory leaflet on claimants' rights. A further head of claim covering residual loss from tilt and other structural distortion was added to the Code of Practice. This fell short of the Commission's full recommendation, which also covered any loss arising from remedied damage. The White Paper announced that an independent review of the practical operation of the compensation system was needed and that the Government had appointed this Committee to examine and report on it.

CHAPTER 3

THE COMPENSATION SYSTEM IN PRACTICE

In identifying the key issues that arise from the operation of the subsidence compensation system, we consider in this chapter the scale and distribution of damage, the way in which both individual and institutional claimants are affected and compensation practice elsewhere.

43. Surface damage from mining subsidence is not confined to the coalfields: it can result also from the working of salt, limestone, ironstone and other minerals. But the deep mining of coal has for many years accounted for the most extensive and serious damage, and this is reflected in the unique body of statute and practice that makes up the subsidence compensation system. We have looked carefully at the extent of subsidence damage and the cost to the Board of its restitution. We have also examined claimants' experience of the compensation system and the issues that concern them in the light of the evidence we have seen and heard, and received in writing. This provides the starting point for considering compensation practice elsewhere and identifying the key issues with which we deal systematically in subsequent chapters.

The Extent of Subsidence Damage

44. The process whereby land subsides and property is damaged is described in detail in Annex B. This illustrates how subsidence tends to manifest itself on the surface as a wave which advances ahead of the coal face, and how the tension and compression it produces can cause surface damage as the wave passes. Some areas experience a succession of such waves as each new coal face is advanced underground. This feature of the subsidence process explains some of the uncertainty about the timing and extent of damage which the system of repair and compensation has to take into account.

45. Some measure of the extent of subsidence damage is given by the total number of new claims received each year by the Board. In 1982/83 this totalled 22,000 compared with 14,000 only two years previously. These figures reflect the number of people prepared to make a claim, as well as the actual amount of damage suffered by the inhabitants of mining areas. It is probable also that the Board's recent disposition to accept wider obligations in this field accounts for some of the increase in the number of claims. The survey which we commissioned suggested that there were significant numbers of households who had suffered damage but did not submit a claim, largely because they considered the damage too slight to be worth the effort of proceeding. The smaller number who suffered appreciable damage and yet did not claim is of concern, but the evidence of the survey does not point to a widespread take-up problem within the system, at least within those areas where mining subsidence is a well known phenomenon. Outside such areas, there may be a problem, although we have no direct evidence of this.

46.   A further measure of the extent of subsidence damage is provided by the cost of subsidence compensation payments to the Board. (The make up of these payments is described in Annex H). This has risen from £6.2 million in 1972/73 to £17 million in 1976/77 and to £90 million in 1982/83 – compared with a decrease in saleable coal output in those same years from 129 million tonnes, to 108 million tonnes, and to 100 million tonnes respectively. In real terms this represents a four fold increase in subsidence costs in ten years. As for the future, we note that the original provision for subsidence compensation in 1983/84 of £102 million has recently been increased very substantially to £230 million, following the Spring Supplementary Estimates. We also note that the Secretary of State for Energy has initiated an enquiry into this increase, largely accounted for by additional provision in one Board Area.

47.   Of the 22,000 new claims received in 1982/83, two thirds were in the North Nottinghamshire, South Nottinghamshire, and North Derbyshire Areas of the Board. These three areas also accounted for almost seventy per cent of total subsidence damage costs in that year, with a large proportion of the remainder being attributable to the Yorkshire coalfield. Relatively small subsidence costs were incurred in the older coalfields of Scotland, South Wales and the North East. It has not been possible on the statistical evidence before us to establish whether this pattern of costs accurately reflects a trend which will continue in future years, since the 1982/83 figures look to be somewhat distorted by the concentration of mining activity under one or two built-up areas. Nevertheless it is significant that very substantial numbers of claims are continuing to be received in those Areas where mining has an assured long term future.

48.   Almost seventy per cent of the total costs of all claims in 1982/83 were for dwelling houses, including local authority houses, and a further fifteen per cent for statutory undertakings and public authorities. Relatively small amounts were paid out on agricultural and industrial claims. In future years the Board expect to mine less under urban areas and more under the low-lying agricultural land in the eastern coalfield, and at a greater depth. We would expect this trend to lead to a slight shift in the overall distribution of types of claim, but, for the foreseeable future, claims on domestic property are likely to continue to provide the main focus of the compensation system.

49.   We also sought to establish the severity of damage in the different Areas, and the costs incurred by each category. The Board, surprisingly, do not differentiate in their accounts between payments for different categories of damage, but at our request they compiled statistics on the number and distribution of cases of "very severe" damage – largely cases where demolition or substantial rebuilding was involved – and listed the collieries mainly responsible. These figures are reproduced in Annex H together with the precise definition used. This definition is more limited than the general definition of very severe damage which amounted in 1982/83 to £8 million, nearly ten per cent of the total cost of all claims. A similar picture emerged in relation to domestic properties, with ten per cent of costs attributable to less than two and a half per cent of claims. At the same time, almost two-thirds of costs for domestic property arose in the North Nottinghamshire Area, primarily from extensive workings under the urban areas of Mansfield and

14

Sutton. In the absence of similar figures for other categories of damage it is not possible to draw firm conclusions from this analysis. The survey which we commissioned in a small number of areas known to have been badly affected by subsidence damage suggested that over twenty five per cent of homes had suffered "appreciable" or "serious" damage, and three per cent "very severe" damage, but we were not able to match these against the costs of restitution. The indications are that the cost of meeting claims arising from the worst categories of damage is disproportionately high, and attributable to relatively few collieries.

50.   It has not been possible to compare the administrative costs of dealing with different categories of claim or to make comparisons of cost between different Areas. The Board do not hold figures showing the annual cost of administering the compensation system, although they have at our request attempted to provide an indication of the way in which they deploy staff dealing with subsidence matters. These details can also be found in Annex H. From them, it is possible to derive an approximate figure of the number of claims dealt with annually by "subsidence" staff in different Areas, together with their average cost. There seems on this evidence to be no apparent match between the deployment of staff effort and the actual workload – in terms of number and cost of claims – although we acknowledge the dangers inherent in any such simple comparison.

The Experience of Claimants

51.   The evidence which we have received has been very substantial. It has come from all parts of the country, although most has originated in the main Yorkshire/Nottinghamshire/Derbyshire coalfield. Only a small volume of correspondence has come from members of the public in Scotland and the North East, which in view of the incidence of damage is not unexpected. There were also a large number of letters from South Wales and from the Western Areas of the Board. We have not sought to explain these variations, although it is quite clear that the attitudes of the Board's staff towards subsidence damage, and the handling of claims, do vary considerably between the Board's Areas and no doubt these are reflected in the responses we have received. An analysis of letters received from members of the public is at Annex E.

52.   Evidence submitted by various institutions and public bodies has been invaluable in our assessment of the compensation system. We have nonetheless made special efforts to obtain the views of individual domestic claimants direct, either in writing, through visits and interview, or by special survey. These efforts have successfully enabled us to hear from people with direct experience of the system. Their concern, almost invariably, has been to see the damage put right quickly and to a reasonable standard, and to secure from the Board a recognition that, through no fault of their own, they have been inconvenienced, to a greater or lesser degree. We have been impressed by the essential reasonableness of the great majority of those who have approached us. Inevitably their comments focus on the shortcomings of the system. We therefore wish to record that many of those who have been affected by subsidence damage appear to be broadly satisfied both with the intent of the legislation and Code of Practice, and also with their treatment by

the Board. Many paid tribute to the Board's officers in the field. This generally accords with our own view.

53. The shortcomings of the present system as seen by claimants are nevertheless worrying, covering as they do a very wide spectrum. Many relate to the way in which the Board carry out their obligations under Statute or the Code of Practice rather than to defects in the statutory provisions themselves. We have little doubt that the main thrust of the existing provisions is right, although some significant gaps remain to be filled.

54. A great deal of dissatisfaction with the system stems in our view from inadequate channels of communication both within the Board and between the Board and individuals – before, during and after subsidence damage has occurred. For example, we were disturbed to find how little advance warning, if any, people were given about mining intentions and about the likelihood of subsidence damage. Sixty five per cent of those in our survey who suffered damage claimed not to have had any prior notification. Of those who were aware of possible future subsidence, almost half had been told by neighbours, with only a quarter (or eight per cent of the total) giving the Board as their source of information. The survey showed that the Board played a significant role in response to enquiries in advising people of their rights, and how to claim once damage had been reported, but almost one in ten of the letters sent to us complained about the difficulty of communicating with the Board; and about the same number spoke of the Board's attitude being sometimes less than helpful. We also noted that poor communications were not confined to relations between claimants and the Board. In some instances it was clear that the local authority and National Coal Board tenants were singularly ill-informed of their position, and we were unimpressed by the quality of communication between a number of claimants and their technical advisers. There is therefore no single cause of poor communications, although the Board quite obviously have a pivotal position in the system and must bear much of the responsibility. We find contradictions in the Board's attitudes in these matters difficult to understand, and in some cases indefensible. They are often generous in putting damage right and in treating people sympathetically, but appear unnecessarily grudging in informing people about the Board's intentions and about their legal rights.

55. Many people expressed concern about the handling of queries and disputes. Seventeen per cent of all past claimants in the survey and thirty seven per cent of current claimants expressed dissatisfaction with negotiations on claims. Not surprisingly many cases revolved around the question of the liability of the Board for damage, particularly in areas where mining activity had taken place over a long period, and where the combination of old workings and a complex geology had confused the picture. We were unhappy with the impression of certainty conveyed by the Board in denying liability in some circumstances, and recognised that faced with such a blunt and often brief denial a claimant might easily decide that it would be pointless to pursue the issue. We doubt whether claimants take such decisions in full knowledge of the avenues available to them when in dispute with the Board.

56. Even where claimants – and their advisers – are aware of these avenues through the Lands Tribunal, the Courts or arbitration provided in the Code of Practice, we formed the clear impression that they were rarely seriously considered, or were felt to be weighted heavily in favour of the Board. During the three year period ending December 1983 only eight claims for coal mining subsidence damage were referred to the Lands Tribunal, the same number to the High Court, five to the County Court and only one to the Sheriff (Scotland only). This reluctance to make use of the available procedures for resolving disputes recurred repeatedly during our enquiries, and has commanded much attention during our subsequent deliberations.

57. The central element of the compensation system is of course the repair of subsidence damage. Eighty seven per cent of past claims in the survey, and a similar proportion of current claims involved repairs. Yet twenty per cent of letters received complained about the standard of repairs, six per cent about the length of time taken to complete them, and an equal number about the attitude and behaviour of contractors. Similar results were obtained from the survey, with about a quarter of claimants reporting that repairs were not to a satisfactory standard, and an equal number pointing out that they were not carried out as quickly as could have been expected. Our own enquiries revealed that in a disturbing number of cases there appeared to be no agreed statement of damage or schedule of repairs available to the claimant and little apparent supervision or subsequent follow up once repairs had been completed. On the evidence of respondents in the survey one third of repair jobs never had a supervisory visit.

58. We recognise that the carrying out of repairs to damaged property is often difficult for the claimant and unappealing to the contractor. In these circumstances it is perhaps surprising that more complaints are not received by the Board. Yet attention is almost incvitably focused on the Board's repair practices as the main plank of the system. On the evidence we have taken, attitudes towards the outcome of repairs are also coloured by the practice of issuing 'stop notices', which effectively defer the completion of proper repairs. Whatever their justification, the use of 'stop notices' often causes confusion and resentment, particularly where they are left in force on a property for a considerable time without adequate explanation. Our survey indicated that nearly a quarter of claimants had 'stop notices' issued, sometimes covering a period of five years or more. We noted with deep concern the length of time some families had endured, without complaint, the discomfort of living in damaged property, only superficially repaired and with no clear idea about when they would see an end to their condition. It seemed to us that in some areas a sensible precaution had become an unfortunate habit.

59. Where damage has been extensive and it is difficult to carry out repairs, families accept the need to move out into temporary accommodation. They naturally wish this to be for as short a time as possible, and for their temporary home to be both comfortable and near to their own home. One in ten of the letters we received mentioned the time people were away from their home and eight per cent of the claimants in the survey had been in temporary accommodation; almost forty per cent of these spent between

eleven and thirty weeks in such accommodation, and thirty per cent were away for longer still. Twenty five per cent of people in the survey also felt that the standard of accommodation was poor, and a significant number mentioned their concern for what was happening to their own home whilst there were away. For example, contractors used vacated houses as stores whilst they carried out repairs elsewhere. Understandably, these worries increase the longer the time away and particularly where there are young children in the family, or where the persons affected are elderly.

60. If subsidence damage and its repair are long drawn-out, particularly after a property is severely affected, stress and strain on the occupants is increased and ill-health can sometimes result. A fifth of letters from the public drew attention to the personal distress suffered by themselves or close relatives or neighbours. We talked to some of those affected ourselves. We were left in no doubt that subsidence damage could indeed be traumatic, and if a person were elderly or already in poor health, the damage and process of repair might be the last straw. More common is the case where repairs are carried out piecemeal apparently at the whim of the contractor, and stress and strain result more from frustration with the contractor than from the extent of damage itself. This is particularly understandable when it may be the second or third time that repairs have been necessary to the same property.

61. When, in a particular area, repairs are not effected for a considerable time, and when on completion their quality is found to be uneven, there is markedly less willingness on the part of claimants to leave repairs to the Board. In these circumstances, claimants may opt to take compensation payments instead and then arrange themselves for the repairs to be done. We received some evidence that this practice was encouraged in certain areas – either because the Board's resources were fully stretched, or because agents had canvassed this particular route. This clearly makes sense providing the repairs are carried out to a proper standard, but we were concerned for the possible consequences for the area, including widespread dereliction, if this were not done.

62. We received a confused picture of the working of the provisions in the Code of Practice for payment over and above repairs. Awareness of these additional provisions is very patchy, and individual claimants are often dependent upon either professional advice or the Board to point them in the right direction. We have no reason to believe that the Board are attempting to avoid their obligations under the Code, but many claimants were unfamiliar with the provisions and unclear as to what might be claimed. It is quite evident, and a cause for concern, that in these circumstances the experienced or well-advised claimant is able to benefit from the Code whereas the inexperienced is not. It may explain some of the grievances expressed about the scope of compensation provision.

63. Relatively few of those affected by subsidence damage contemplate moving to another area – although eleven per cent of respondents in the survey claimed to have done so. However, a damaged property is likely to suffer some fall in value, even though it will be repaired in due course, and this would represent a loss to those moving away. The Board do purchase

such properties or make top-up payments in certain circumstances, but they are naturally anxious to avoid a major excursion into the property market. Our attention therefore focused on the criteria adopted by the Board to define these hardship cases and on whether people were being treated equitably.

64.   The representations we have received on loss of property value range from the specific – where people have had difficulty in selling their houses after subsidence repair for example – to the general – where there has been a "blighting" effect on the local housing market in advance of mining taking place. Six per cent of letters from the public mentioned specifically a loss in value, and a similar number difficulty in selling. We also received a number of letters expressing concern about valuation in cases where the Board were approached as to purchase or compensation. But it has been difficult to obtain objective evidence in this general area, and therein lies part of the difficulty in considering the adequacy of existing provisions. We believe that in the traditional coalfields there is little discernible long term loss in property values as these have long reflected liability to subsidence damage, but there may be some permanent loss in previously unworked areas. This is an added reason for considering whether there is an identifiable permanent loss in value, and if so whether it should be included amongst possible extensions to the scope of compensation provision.

65.   Each of these aspects of the compensation scheme provides a potential source of difficulty for the claimant, and it is therefore understandable that many claimants choose to seek specialist advice on how to pursue a claim against the Board. Such advice appears to be widely appreciated by claimants, and often welcomed by the Board since it may simplify negotiations. The Board however expressed their concern to us about the activities of some agents and technical advisers in certain coalfield areas. Examples were quoted of agents actively canvassing for mining subsidence business, preparing claims on the basis of a standard check list of damage without any attempt being made to differentiate between dilapidation and mining subsidence damage, and then submitting batches of delayed claims. This was certainly the case in one area which we visited, and we were unhappy about the possible consequences both for the Board and for claimants. We remain uncertain, however, about how widespread a problem this is, or is likely to become, and how far the conduct of practitioners is amenable to direct regulation.

Non-domestic Claimants: Agriculture, Industry, Public Utilities and Local Authorities.

66.   Much of what we have heard and seen of the working of the compensation system as it applies to domestic dwellings has been repeated in the evidence submitted by agricultural, commercial, and industrial interests, by public utilities, and by local authorities in their role as developers. But their comments have in general been more muted, reflecting the special efforts and agreements reached by the Board in this more "institutionalised" field. In general the larger bodies expressed their overall satisfaction with the arrangements they had concluded with the Board, ranging from discussions

about mining plans and precautionary measures to compensation following damage and we formed the impression that there were relatively few issues where agreement could not be reached with the Board albeit after what might be a long bargaining period. Most of the difficulties raised by these bodies were different only in scale from the evident problems of domestic householders, and would therefore be tackled effectively by improvements to the compensation system generally. Satisfaction with the scheme does however appear to depend over much on relative bargaining powers and we have therefore been particularly anxious to review the position of the small agricultural or industrial enterprise.

67. The main concern amongst the farming community has been to ensure no permanent loss of the productive potential of agricultural land. Their evidence especially emphasised the need for full discussion in advance of mine working, for adequate precautionary and preventive works, and for full restitution of the condition of the land should subsidence damage occur. Where it was not possible to restore the land to its previous condition and productive potential, it was argued that compensation should cover not only loss of current production – such as crops – but loss attributable to a decline in the overall effectiveness of the farm as a unit. This emphasis was reflected in the main thrust of the arguments heard at the planning inquiries in the Selby and North East Leicestershire coalfields. In practice it focuses attention on the practical problems of land drainage, particularly the fine balance that exists in many of the areas underlain by the eastern coalfield between land suitable for profitable farming and that vulnerable to extensive flooding. Day-to-day relations between the Board and farmers repeated more exactly the position we found in relation to domestic households, although there are special problems associated with temporary accommodation should a farm house be severely damaged.

68. We received relatively little evidence from industry or from commercial undertakings. We take this to reflect general satisfaction with the working of the compensation system. It was confirmed to a considerable extent by the visits we made to a number of factories. We were impressed by the efforts made by the Board and management to ensure that subsidence damage was minimised and production uninterrupted. There would appear no widespread support for specific compensation for loss of production or profit, although small firms and small commercial premises have less scope for avoiding such losses. Certain types of enterprise are also less able to cope with repairs without disrupting business and staff, and the uncertainty about the timing of subsidence can be an unwelcome additional investment risk.

69. Many public utilities have special powers under legislation that relate to the withdrawal of support, and may have negotiated special agreements for compensation. This is a particular tradition stemming from the Mining Codes, where support is retained under sensitive surface structures such as railways and pipelines in return for compensation, and there would appear little call to modify these arrangements. Where such agreements are less comprehensive – particularly between the water and drainage authorities and the Board – there is some cause for concern in the "grey" areas where liability or compensation payments may be disputed. This particularly applies to historic damage to

sewers and pipelines, and to damage caused by the escape of water, for example, from fractured mains. In addition, all public utilities need to plan their investment a long time in advance, and, in view of the importance such infrastructure plays in both public and private surface development, there was some anxiety that mining and utility investment proposals should be brought forward in a way that enables both to proceed in concert as far as is possible.

70.   Similar points were put to us by the local authorities in their role as both developers and planning authorities. Failure to coordinate mining plans with development plans can lead to unnecessary costs at a time when pressure on financial resources is substantial, and a number of examples were given to us. As in the case of agricultural drainage systems or public utilities, additional expenditure is also incurred where higher maintenance costs follow from repairs or restitution, although the main issue here seems to be the form in which compensation is paid by the Board rather than whether compensation should be paid at all. A particular case was put to us by a number of housing authorities who had incurred additional expenditure on precautionary measures and in replacing demolished local authority housing. In these circumstances they felt that due allowance should be made for these higher costs in their investment allocations from the Department of the Environment.

Compensation in Other Fields

71.   In formulating the main issues upon which we focus our attention in the remainder of our report, we have had regard to the principles of repair and compensation elsewhere, in so far as they hold lessons for mining subsidence. In a closely analogous area, the pumping of brine in Cheshire, compensation is set and administered by a special Board, and in other areas, such as a motorway, airport, or other public projects, provision is largely governed by the Land Compensation Act 1973 or the Land Compensation (Scotland) Act 1973. In considering these systems, we have followed the Working Party whose recommendations formed the basis of the current Code of Practice. We have noted in particular that the effects of mining subsidence are more intrusive upon families within their home than those arising from other forms of development, although, unlike the effects of a motorway for example, they may be relatively short-lived. In seeking to balance these factors we have recognised the need to consider the rights of both the surface owner and the Board. Here again there would appear to be no clear-cut dividing line between the different interests.

72.   We have also considered briefly the scope of compensation provision for mining subsidence damage in the Federal Republic of Germany and in France. In the Federal Republic, restitution is covered by the Mining Code, introduced in 1982. It includes, in the case of damage to land and fixed plant and equipment, compensation for the proven cost of interrupted production and lost profits. The Federal Republic's law also requires mining companies to reimburse developers for preventive and precautionary measures. These measures need not be taken if the cost is disproportionate to the reduction in the risk of subsidence damage, although the mining company may then be required to pay compensation for the loss in value of the land, or to buy the land, if it is effectively sterilised as a result.

73.   There is no specific legislation covering subsidence compensation in France, but if cause and effect can be proven the mining company is liable under the Civil Code. Compensation payments are normally preferred to repair, although the scale of damage is much less than in this country. Compensation may cover liability for loss of profit or for disturbance arising directly from the damage or its repair, but appears to fall short of compensation for full consequential loss.

Key Issues

74.   On the basis of the evidence presented to us, and against this background of compensation provision elsewhere, we have identified six key issues. These both encompass our concern and provide a systematic framework within which we assess the arguments for and against change, and present our recommendations. They are:

  (i)   prediction and prevention – the extent to which subsidence damage can be predicted, limited and perhaps prevented;

 (ii)   notification and publicity – what sort of information should be provided in advance of mining taking place and to whom;

(iii)   the repair of damage – what balance should be struck between repair and monetary compensation; how can repairs be carried out more efficiently and effectively;

 (iv)   the scope of compensation provision – what additional areas of compensation are needed, if any;

  (v)   disputes – how adequate are the provisions for resolving disputes and possible improvements;

 (vi)   the statutory framework, management and monitoring – what should be the main elements of statute and associated codes; how can management practices be improved, and performance monitored.

75.   We address each of these key issues in turn against the background of principles outlined in paragraphs 8–12, and having regard to the broad costs and benefits they imply.

CHAPTER 4

PREDICTION AND PREVENTION

We examine in this chapter the scope for improving the prediction of subsidence, and for reducing surface damage by means of changes to mine design and by the use of precautionary and preventive measures.

76.   We recognise that some degree of subsidence, leading to damage to buildings, highways, services and drainage systems, is an unavoidable effect of modern deep mining operations. We also recognise that it frequently does not make good economic sense to attempt widespread preventive measures. Much of the damage is of a minor nature and is quickly repaired at no great inconvenience to those affected. It is nonetheless clear to us that if new mining proposals are to be publicly acceptable, the Board will need to demonstrate to a greater extent than in the past that they have fully considered the effects of subsidence on the surface and that they intend to take all reasonable measures to keep surface damage to a minimum. We consider it most unlikely that public interest in these matters will recede, notwithstanding the improvements we recommend to repair and compensation practice. Their importance has been effectively demonstrated at the two public inquiries into mining proposals at Selby and in the North East Leicestershire coalfield. We have therefore considered carefully how far it is reasonable to expect the Board to place greater emphasis in their mine planning on measures designed to minimise surface damage in advance of working particular seams.

Prediction

77.   The Board's ability to take into account the effects of subsidence in assessing proposals for new investment capacity, and in considering the scope for precautionary and preventive measures, hinges on accurate prediction of when and where subsidence will occur and with what effect on surface structures. Much has been achieved, and the Board have an enviable international reputation for their work in this field.

78.   Accurate predictions of ground movement, particularly of vertical settlement, are possible where geological conditions are straightforward, and we are assured that the Board's methods are continually being updated as more and better information becomes available. Damage results however more from the stresses and strains induced by the subsidence process than from vertical settlement as such, and these effects are more difficult to predict. Local faulting, the presence of old mineral workings, the precise nature of the strata between the coal seam(s) and the surface, all affect the accuracy of ground movement predictions. We are concerned that the predictive models used by the Board do not appear to take sufficient account of these factors where they vary markedly between coalfield areas. More accurate ground movement prediction, particularly of horizontal strain, is important if the worst effects of subsidence damage are to be avoided, and we **recommend** that the Board should carry out more detailed geological surveys

in areas where there is *prima facie* evidence to suggest that ground movement is likely to be appreciable.

79.   Substantial improvement in prediction methods is dependent upon accurate geological maps indicating in particular the location of faults and other structural features known to have a significant influence on the subsidence profile at the surface. We understand that most of the maps that relate to the coalfields were published many years ago, and are recognised by most specialist geologists as often being incorrect or seriously misleading. We cannot accept this with equanimity. If surface damage is to be kept to a minimum it is essential that the geological maps for coalfield areas are brought up to date as quickly as possible. We **recommend** that the British Geological Survey should urgently investigate the reliability of the 1 : 10000 and 1 : 10560 series covering the coalfields, and subsequently agree with the Departments of the Environment and Energy, and the National Coal Board, a programme for their revision, incorporating all the information available from plans of abandoned mines.

80.   We recognise that it is more difficult to predict accurately the extent of damage to surface structures or infrastructures, whether buildings, services, or drainage systems. Damage in these cases depends not only on the nature and amount of ground movement, but also on the size, shape, orientation, design and construction of these structures, and the degree to which they are secured to the ground at foundation level. Nevertheless, the Board assure us that it is usually possible to obtain a reasonable forecast of the degree of damage to a typical structure for the purpose of estimating the cost of repair, inconvenience to occupants, or possible interruption of use in the case of a factory or school. This does not mean that the Board are always able to predict the precise extent of damage to a specific property in a particular locality. But it indicates that much can be done to predict and to reduce damage. This is done when circumstances are thought by the Board to warrant it, for example, where public safety is concerned, where there is a building of particular historical significance, or where there is sensitive industrial machinery and plant. We support these priorities, but **recommend** that where the board identify other sensitive community targets – for example, closely-knit residential neighbourhoods – they should similarly aim to establish the likely effect of subsidence on a sample of properties in the area and undertake appropriate preventive works.

81.   The Board, together with the authorities concerned, are also able to predict damage to linear structures, such as railway lines, sewers, highways and pipelines with increasing accuracy. Public safety considerations are such that we consider there is already every possible incentive for the Board to secure further improvements, and to ensure that the necessary measures are taken. The Board should also make further improvements in prediction in relation to land drainage systems, which are particularly vulnerable to changes in gradient that may be occasioned by subsidence. Experience so far in relation to land drainage systems has shown that measures taken to secure the main water courses and internal drainage systems are usually sufficient to ensure that large areas of agricultural land can be undermined without adverse effects on individual field drainage systems. Where the receiving

watercourse has not subsided to the same degree as the field drainage systems, the re-laying of field drains has been essential. We agree with the National Farmers' Union that as mining increasingly takes place beneath low-lying agricultural land there will be a greater risk of a permanent loss of land of good quality. It will therefore be important to ensure that accurate predictions of the effect of subsidence on all drainage systems are available before mining begins, as a basis for discussion of preventive and remedial measures.

82.   We emphasise that it is in the Board's own interest to improve the methods and techniques of prediction in so far as this enables a proper assessment to be made of the costs of extracting coal. We understand that the expected subsidence costs are now assessed in broad terms as part of the five-year operational programme prepared for each colliery, and in more detail when preparing individual face layouts. We welcome this, and **recommend** that the Board issue further guidance to Areas as to the way in which subsidence costs should be incorporated in the appraisal of all mining proposals.

83.   Incorporating subsidence damage costs in this way should help to ensure that the environmental costs of extracting coal are properly considered by the Board when making mining investment decisions. We have nonetheless seen examples of subsidence damage where the effects on community and family life have been, to our mind, so devastating as to be unacceptable. In some of the cases we have seen that the damaging effects were the result of a particular combination of geological conditions, and were not wholly predictable. In others the damage could have been foreseen. We **recommend** that where the Board predict that severe and very severe surface damage is likely to occur, they should not normally extract the coal unless they are able to reduce the scale of that damage by means of preventive action to surface structures or by modifications to underground lay-out.

84.   This approach would mean that some coal could not be extracted economically at all. We consider that the circumstances in which this is likely to be the case are infrequent. There is considerable scope in the newer coalfields for modifying mine design so as to minimise surface damage whilst retaining acceptable production levels. In the older coalfields there may be less scope for this, and the result may be that some coal is not worked. We understand that some cases of severe subsidence damage have followed from the extraction of the last workable reserves of an older colliery. We recognise that there may be good social, and occasionally economic, reasons for mining this coal, but believe strongly that where collieries are near the end of their working life the Board should do so only after weighing in full the costs and benefits to the whole community of working the remaining reserves. If they decide to proceed, every effort should be made to inform those likely to be affected and to anticipate and deal comprehensively with the resultant damage and distress.

85.   We have considered how far a tightening of planning control might help to ensure that these wider social costs are taken fully into account in all new investments. Where the Board require planning permission in order to open a

new mine or, exceptionally, a new seam in an existing mine, we **recommend** that these factors should be given full weight in determining an application. But local authorities have made the point forcibly to us that most new mining investment takes place under the General Development Orders (GDO) which confer on the Board, *inter alia,* planning permission to work new reserves underground at mines opened before July 1948. This means that there is no obvious mechanism by which the broader costs and benefits to the local community of new mining investment can be considered, and discussed openly in the way we consider necessary. We believe that this is not in the public interest. We suggest that there is a strong case for bringing new underground workings under effective planning control. We understand that the Environment Departments are currently reviewing Class XX (Class XVII in Scotland) of the GDO, and we **recommend** that they should explore ways of achieving tighter control over new underground development to enable planning authorities to consider properly the effects of possible subsidence and the extent to which these can be prevented or ameliorated.

86.   There are three main ways by which surface damage can be minimised:
   (i)   by modifying mine design;
  (ii)   by carrying out preventive works to existing structures;
 (iii)   by taking precautionary measures in new surface development.

We explore each of these in turn.

Modifications to Mine Design

87.   Almost all deep-mine coal output is produced by the mechanised long-wall method, and a growing proportion is won by retreat mining. Although new techniques of winning coal will continue to be developed it is unlikely that these will lead to any real alternative to long-wall methods in the foreseeable future. This means that surface subsidence as presently experienced will remain a feature of modern coal mining for many years to come, although the severity of damage to buildings and structures may be less as mining is largely concentrated on the deeper seams beneath less densely populated areas. Alternative techniques affecting the method of cutting at the coal face, or the means of transport below ground, are unlikely to affect subsidence patterns at the surface, unless they include ways in which the coal extracted can be replaced by material of equivalent strength. The report of the Underground Stowage Working Party [1] indicates that under certain circumstances surface subsidence can be reduced by up to fifty per cent by the stowage of colliery spoil in the void created by the extracting of coal, but it is clear that this is no simple panacea for the subsidence problem. There remain considerable technical obstacles, and important health and safety factors, yet to be overcome. Underground stowage is however clearly an option in limited circumstances, and we support the recommendations of the Working Party for further research designed to extend the range of possibilities.

---

[1] North East Leicestershire Prospect. Working Party on Underground Stowage – Final Report. Department of the Environment. October 1983.

88.   Other measures which can be taken at the mine design stage include partial extraction, the retention of pillars of support, variation in the geometry of working panels and "harmonic" mining, whereby the effects from different panels are applied to cancel each other out. Each of these methods has both advantages and disadvantages. We do not consider it appropriate to examine these in detail (although Annex B provides a fuller explanation of the terms), but we would expect their use to be fully considered by the Board in their appraisal of mining proposals. To some extent this is already the Board's practice. They have indicated to us that in some fifty five recent cases mining plans were modified to reduce subsidence damage. Designed partial extraction systems in particular have been successful in many areas where it has been necessary to minimise surface damage. Typically these systems can allow fifty per cent of a seam to be extracted under built-up areas, and up to seventy per cent in certain other circumstances. This has been done successfully, for example, beneath Coventry. And at Whitwick Colliery near Coalville working has been carried out by a series of narrow headings with narrow intervening pillars. We **recommend** that the lessons learnt from experiments of this kind be disseminated widely within the Board, and encouragement given to their use in areas sensitive to subsidence.

Preventive Works to Existing Structures

89.   The Board have powers under Section 4 of the 1957 Act to execute works on existing property which would prevent the occurrence or reduce the extent of subsidence damage. Such measures either allow relative movement between parts of the structure, or reduce the degree of ground movement being transmitted to and through it. Similarly, service pipes, sewers and trunk pipelines can be modified by the insertion of telescopic and flexible joints, and by excavation to relieve stress during the period of subsidence.

90.   In deciding whether to carry out preventive works the Board must weigh the cost of such measures against the risk to public safety and the cost of subsequent compensation. The Board give priority to preventive works where public safety might be at risk, and where important historic or public buildings might be affected by subsidence damage. Preventive works are also commonly carried out to sensitive industrial premises and plant. Preventive works to domestic property – involving cutting slots in the building and the excavation of trenches for example – are worthwhile in certain circumstances but can in themselves be disruptive and disfiguring. We believe that these considerations should be put to the public and discussed with them. The Board have agreed to full public discussion of the scope of preventive measures, and we **recommend** that this should take place following the notice of approach which we describe in Chapter 5.

Precautionary Measures in New Surface Development

91.   There is widespread support for the more extensive incorporation of precautionary measures in the design and construction of new buildings and surface structures. There is little consensus however amongst those giving

evidence on two key related questions – who should decide whether precautionary measures should be taken, and if so who should pay. A long-standing consultation procedure under Article 15(1)(d) of the GDO 1977 (Article 13(1)(e) of the Scottish GDO 1981) requires local planning authorities to consult the Board before granting planning permission for buildings in an area of coal working which has been notified by the Board to the authority. The Board are entitled under Schedule 1 of the 1975 Act to recommend precautionary measures in the construction of foundations where they consider it appropriate, so as to minimise or avoid the effects of subsidence. If the Board choose to insist that such measures are taken, then they must meet the extra cost incurred by the developer. In practice the Board rarely insist, limiting their comments to the planning authority to a general statement of the desirability of taking such measures. Some local authorities nonetheless require the developer, as a condition of planning permission, to incorporate specific precautionary measures in the design of buildings: others simply pass on the Board's advice to the developer, who may or may not choose to act upon it. We understand that in many traditional mining areas precautionary measures are taken as a matter of course by local authority and private developers, and the costs are borne by them, but this is not always the case. The Department of the Environment recognise that the position is unsatisfactory and are currently reviewing their advice in relation to development on unstable land generally.

92.   We understand that it is the Department's view that the stability of the land can be a material factor in deciding whether planning permission should be granted for any proposed development. It is therefore for the local planning authority to consider whether permission should be refused because the development is premature or whether precautionary measures should be imposed as a planning condition, in which case the developer would be expected to meet the costs in full.

93.   We have considered carefully whether in coal mining areas the full costs of precautionary measures specified in the grant of planning permission should fall on the developer, or whether in view of the possible savings on subsequent damage costs, the Board should pay all or part of those costs. The Board take the view that local authorities should require appropriate precautionary measures to be taken when planning permission is given for new development, and that the costs should be carried by the developer. Evidence from local authorities and the Law Society suggests that the costs should fall on the Board.

94.   We believe that precautionary measures should be taken where the local planning authority consider it appropriate. We also believe that the only realistic way forward is on the basis of a sharing of costs between the developer and the Board. The developer – and the subsequent occupier – benefit from the additional protection against ground movement not directly attributable to the mining of coal. There should also be some incentive on the developer to properly consider the development risks. The Board, for their part, stand to save later subsidence repair costs. This formula recognises that there are conflicting interests in the land, and although these should theoretically be reflected in the price paid for the surface interest, in practice

this rarely applies or has been eroded by the passage of time. We therefore **recommend** that the additional costs of incorporating precautionary measures required by the local planning authority, after consultation with the developer and the Board, should be shared between the two parties on a basis to be settled between them, taking into account the provisions made for development in approved plans and the stage reached in mining plans. In support of this view, we note that the costs of preventive and precautionary measures incurred by some statutory undertakings are frequently negotiated on a shared basis, taking into account the 'betterment' so conferred on the undertaking and the benefits to the Board. We envisage a similar negotiated agreement on specific projects between the developer and the Board. If no such agreement can be reached, the matter should be settled through the disputes procedure recommended in Chapter 8.

95. This process of apportioning the additional costs of precautionary measures should also apply to new local authority development in coal mining areas. Some of these additional costs would therefore be met by the Board. The rest should be reflected in the capital expenditure allocations made by central government each year to local authorities. It would be difficult to identify a specific element in each allocation for subsidence precautions, but the Departments concerned should ensure that their procedures give full weight to these factors. Central government should also be prepared to adjust individual allocations during the course of a year should severe subsidence damage to an area require an unexpected rebuilding programme. This would apply particularly to housing investment allocations made by the Environment Departments.

96. Local planning authorities can also make proposals as to the siting or phasing of development where this seems sensible. Where development is deferred because of the Board's mining plans we do not believe that the Board should be liable to pay compensation. It is for the local planning authority, and other public bodies, to consider how far such deferment is reasonable in the light of the improved information on mining intentions we believe should be available to them. Similarly, where development programmes have to be adapted to accommodate unforeseen changes in mine plans we consider that such changes should be regarded as a normal investment risk, and that the Board should not be liable to pay compensation.

CHAPTER 5

NOTIFICATION AND PUBLICITY

We examine in this chapter the ways in which local authorities, major developers, individual households and prospective purchasers might be alerted to the Board's mining intentions and to their rights under the compensation scheme.

97. A common theme running through the written and oral evidence we have received has been dissatisfaction with the level of information provided by the Board in relation to their mining intentions and to claimants' rights to compensation. This issue was raised by the Commission on Energy and the Environment in 1981, and the Government's White Paper in response to their report recorded agreement with the Board on a number of new notification and publicity measures. These had not been introduced at the time of writing, although we understand that this is to be done very soon.

98. In our opinion the current piecemeal availability of the Board's mining intentions, and the inadequate guidance given to the public as to their rights to compensation should subsidence damage occur, are largely responsible for much of the evident public ignorance and concern regarding the compensation system. Where damage has occurred to domestic property the absence of prior warning has produced both anger and anxiety. It has also led to a measure of disenchantment with the Board in some Areas, and has fostered accusations that mining has taken place with little apparent regard for the effects on the people who live there. Local authorities and other public bodies with longer-term investment programmes often feel that they have been given insufficient warning of mining intentions, and that as a result they have incurred needless expenditure. We have considerable sympathy with these criticisms, and believe that the Board should demonstrate far greater concern in advance of development for those likely to be affected by their activities below ground. A caring attitude should extend as much to the period before mining as to the period following subsidence damage.

Purpose of Notification

99. Notification of proposed and current mine workings should be designed to alert to the possibility of subsidence damage both those who have a need to know (for example, local authorities, public utilities and other major developers) and those who have a right to know (for example, those whose property might be affected). This would facilitate the sensible deferment of expenditure, whether large capital projects or simple household improvements and decorations. We are not impressed with the argument that more and earlier information would cause planning blight or untoward personal anxiety. Much depends on how that information is conveyed. We believe that the public are sufficiently accustomed to receiving and sorting informatiom from a variety of different sources to make good use of what is made available to them.

30

100.   There is a further justification for better notification. Irrespective of the precise interpretation of the Board's responsibility to repair damaged property – to which we return in Chapter 6 – the lack of information about the state of any given property before damage occurs contributes to disputes about the liability of the Board and the adequacy of subsequent repairs. Adequate prior notification of mining plans would provide householders in particular with an opportunity to take advice, and to commission a survey in advance of working, thus materially assisting both the claimant and the Board to assess attributable damage.

101.   At present the Board give information to the public about deep-mining in two ways: through publication of formal notices in newspapers either under Section 2 of the Coal Industry Act 1975 or as part of good practice, and through answers to individual enquiries of the Board, amounting to more than one hundred thousand in 1983. At the same time as the formal Section 2 notices are published the Board must serve a copy on each local planning authority for the area to which the notice relates. In addition, the Board have concluded special arrangements with some local authorities and public undertakings whereby their longer-term mining intentions are passed to those bodies and discussed as necessary. These arrangements have proved most valuable, and we have considered whether they should be put on a more formal footing, and made more generally available.

Mining Intentions – alerting local authorities and major developers

102.   The Board's five-year mining plans for each colliery are inevitably subject to frequent modification and alteration. They are produced and updated annually for the Board's internal planning purposes, and it is right that this should provide their main justification. Informal arrangements already exist whereby these plans are made available to local authorities in the South and West Yorkshire coalfield areas, in order to help them with their new forward planning and development programmes. We believe this to be a valuable exercise, which should not be totally dependent as at present on the good will of the officers concerned. We **recommend** that the Board's five-year colliery plans should be made available on a statutory basis to the mineral planning authorities (in Scotland, to the general or district planning authorities), and updated annually. Such plans should set out, on an Ordnance Survey plan of appropriate scale (usually 1:10000), the under-ground workings proposed for the ensuing twelve months and the seams and areas proposed to be worked over a period of not less than the following four years. At least twelve months before a coal face becomes operational the Board should issue to the appropriate County and District Councils (and equivalent in Scotland and Wales) a notice of approach showing the outline of proposed workings and approximate dates of working.

103.   Using these plans sensibly requires careful interpretation and regular discussion with the Area concerned. Where adjustments are made to plans these need to be notified to local authorities, and if necessary discussed with them in advance. Although mineral planning authorities would eventually develop an expertise which could be helpful to other local authorities in their area, and to other public and private developers, we do not consider that they

should take the lead in interpreting and explaining the Board's five-year plans. This is first and foremost a job for the Board. To this end, we **recommend** that the Board should establish, where requested by local interests, Technical Liaison Committees, similar to that established at Selby. The Committees should include the mineral and local planning authorities, public utilities, and other interests as appropriate – for example, the National Farmers' Union in agricultural areas. They should meet at least annually, and usually more frequently, to discuss the updated five-year plans, their interpretation, any modifications to existing plans, and where appropriate, the scope and timing of precautionary or preventive measures.

104.   Copies of the five year plans should be placed for public inspection in local authority offices throughout mining areas, and inquiries should be referred to the Board's local Area Office. It is for the Board to determine whether these display points should be manned by their officials on particular days, but we would expect some such arrangements to be made wherever there is active local concern about mining plans and possible subsidence damage.

Mining Intentions – alerting householders

105.   Our enquiries have revealed widespread discontent amongst householders about the lack of prior warning of mining and possible subsidence damage. We find the criticism of the Board on this account justified in view of the generally predictable damage and distress that can result from mining operations. Following publication of the White Paper, the Board, in recognition of this concern, are expected to extend the notification procedures currently limited to Section 2 of the 1975 Act. A new notice of intention to mine, covering areas recently mined by the Board and those where it is intended to mine in the near future, is to be published annually in local papers, usually on a parish basis. It is intended, we understand, that the new notice should remind people that in the event of subsidence damage they have rights under legislation and the Code of Practice. At the same time the Department of Energy are to issue a new leaflet explaining those rights. At the time of writing our Report neither the notice or leaflet has been finalised, and we are therefore unable to judge whether they meet in full the undertakings given by the Board. Both may need to be revised in the light of decisions on our Report, and this should be made clear in the explanatory leaflet.

106.   We have however serious reservations about the value of press notices, whether supplemented or not by further information supplied on request, in meeting the evident widespread demand for a more positive approach in advance of damage. An annual notice will cover a large geographical area (twenty or more parishes might be listed) and be imprecise as to timing and likely damage. Even extensive local newspaper coverage will not guarantee that notices are read and the information properly digested, or that individuals likely to be affected by subsidence are well-informed of their rights. The annual notice, as currently proposed, might be improved by indicating the steps the Board intend to take before mining starts – for example, by arranging local meetings to discuss mining plans and action to be

taken in the event of subsidence damage – and by posting this in prominent places in the areas to be affected. It might also include the telephone number of a specific contact within the Area Office. We believe, however, that the Board should be required to take further steps to notify individual householders within the subsidence sphere of influence, usually two to three months prior to undermining.

107. The precise method of notification should be a matter for the Board to decide in consultation with the local authority concerned. Normally the notification should include the delivery of a standard leaflet written as simply as possible to each household in the affected area giving the expected timing of the workings, an indication that subsidence damage may occur, and a specific contact point within the Area office. The explanatory leaflet from the Department of Energy should also be attached. In areas where subsidence damage is expected to be minimal, or where a notice to similar effect has recently been served, the Board should consult and agree with the district authority some other suitable method of notification. We accept that in some extreme cases, mining activity may need to go ahead in advance of individual notification. In that event notification should take place as soon as possible thereafter. In those few cases where notification has been carried out, and mining is subsequently suspended or abandoned, then further notification will be required although not necessarily in the same form.

108. We have considered how far it would be reasonable for the Board to indicate the likely severity of damage at this stage. We recognise that detailed assessments for each property would not be realistic, but we have already taken the view that in the exceptional circumstances where mining is to take place notwithstanding the likelihood of severe and very severe damage occurring, the Board should take steps to warn individual households and to prepare for tackling the expected damage. It follows that we believe it practicable to give a broad indication of likely severity of damage, and that the Board should consider doing so in the light of experience with the new procedures we propose.

109. We are quite clear then that more needs to be done to alert householders to the Board's mining intentions and to their rights should subsidence damage occur. We therefore **recommend** that the Board should be required by statute to:

   a. publish and display annual notices in all areas to be affected by mining developments; and

   b. not more than three months prior to undermining, and in consultation with the district authority, inform householders within the subsidence zone of influence of the timing of the workings, and of their rights in the event of damage occurring.

Within this framework it is right that there should be scope for varying practice to suit local circumstances and administrative convenience. We have allowed for this is suggesting some variation in the precise method of household notification to be adopted, which we **recommend** should be elaborated in a revised Code of Practice. The new measures should be introduced on a pilot basis in the first instance, in full co-operation with the local district authority concerned. This would have the benefit of helping to identify any administrative problems as well as the most effective methods to deploy.

Mining Enquiries

110.   It is important that the benefits arising from improved notification and publicity about the Board's mining intentions should be available to those considering moving to a mining area as well as to those already living there. At present the Board respond to a large number of individual enquiries and, in order to rationalise this process, they and the Law Society have been discussing for some considerable time the possible use of a standard form of mining search addressed to the Board which could be used by prospective purchasers of property in mining areas. We welcome this initiative, but regret that it has not yet been possible to reach agreement on the content of the form. We **recommend** that the Government should bring the two parties together with the aim of reaching early agreement.

111.   The regular use of a standard inquiry form would be a great help to prospective purchasers. It should include a question about previous mining subsidence claims on a property. Our attention has been drawn to a number of cases where new owners have made claims against the Board only to be told that the damage was the subject of an earlier settled claim. In some cases that settlement has been in the form of cash compensation rather than repair, and it is clear that the repairs have not been properly or fully carried out by the previous owner. We address the problem of failure to repair more fully in the next chapter, but for the protection of prospective purchasers we **recommend** that the Board should be required to register each future settled claim on a property with the District Council as though it were a local land charge. Details of the settlement need not be recorded, but the authority would be able to disclose to a properly interested party the fact that there had been a subsidence claim. It would then be for the purchaser to decide whether to make further enquiries of the Board before completing the transaction.

112.   These arrangements would not provide a substitute for the detailed mining reports which prospective purchasers or developers currently commission from the Board for a fee. We would expect the improved procedures to reduce the need for such requests, but there will remain circumstances where a detailed report is required and we think it right that the Board should continue to make a suitable charge for this advice.

CHAPTER 6

THE REPAIR OF SUBSIDENCE DAMAGE

In this chapter we examine the balance between repair and compensation payments, and explore ways in which the repair of subsidence damage can be improved.

113.   The prime concern of the overwhelming majority of those affected by subsidence is that the damage so caused should be put right as quickly as possible and to a high standard. The subsidence compensation system, as at present constituted, has been designed to meet this concern. In many cases it does so. But as we have noted in Chapter 3 there are a number of serious shortcomings in the system which need to be rectified. The recommendations which follow are designed to redress these shortcomings, and build, wherever possible, on the many examples of good practice which we found in the course of our visits. In doing so, we have found it helpful to have regard to the sequence of events involved in the processing of a claim, as illustrated in Annex C.

Repairs or Compensation?

114.   It is the Board's general policy to repair subsidence damage rather than pay cash compensation. In a minority of cases entitlement to compensation derives from a claimant's title to the property and they may, if they prefer, reject the Board's offer to repair in favour of a cash settlement of the claim. Otherwise, where a claim is made under the 1957 Act or other legislation, it is for the Board to decide whether repairs should be carried out or compensation paid. In some areas of extensive damage the Board may not always be able to deal quickly with repair work and may therefore offer cash payments instead. We came across a number of such areas where compensation payments have increasingly been made instead of carrying out repairs. There has, however, been almost unanimous agreement amongst those giving evidence that the emphasis on repairs should remain a central feature of the compensation system and, where possible, it should be strengthened. We agree. It is in the public interest that subsidence damage should be repaired or put right wherever practicable, so that the nation's housing stock is maintained, dereliction and blight are avoided, and those living in mining areas are assured that their environment is not to be sacrificed in the interest of the nation's need for coal. We **recommend** that, as and when subsidence legislation is consolidated, the prime need for repair is emphasised, with the alternative of a compensation payment available to claimants only in exceptional circumstances.

115.   So that damage should be repaired quickly it is important that the initial process of submitting a claim should be as simple and effective as possible. It is anomalous that special forms are required in order to submit a claim under the 1957 Act, but not under other legislation. What is needed is a single comprehensive legal notice of damage to supplement the informal notice which we understand the Board to be considering as part of their

annual notices (para 105). It is important that claims submitted some time after the occurrence of damage are not ruled out on the grounds that they have been received beyond some arbitrary time period. Regulations made under the 1957 Act require claims to be submitted within two months of the damage becoming apparent, although this can be extended on appeal to the Board and/or the Secretary of State for Energy. In practice the Board rarely insist on strict compliance. This is a sensible interpretation, but nonetheless we **recommend** that claims should be received by the Board at any time, and should not be restricted by the Limitation Acts. Within, say, three years of the date when damage should reasonably have been apparent to the claimant the onus would generally be on the Board to prove that subsidence was not the cause of the damage. After three years, the onus of proof would transfer to the claimant. We do not believe that in the event this more open commitment would mean much of a change from existing practice in submitting claims, since it will remain strongly in the interests of the claimant to make a claim quickly. But it would recognise the practical difficulties of distinguishing and reacting to subsidence damage.

116. Emphasis on repair as against a compensation payment focuses attention on the standards of repair. There is some confusion between the obligation to ensure that the property is made 'reasonably fit ..' under the 1957 Act and the repairs are 'to the reasonable satisfaction of the claimant ...' under the 1975 Act. We doubt whether these slightly different obligations on the Board give rise in themselves to a serious deficiency in the quality of repair carried out. The Board assures us that the spirit of the 1975 Act is generally applied. We take the view that it would be helpful to harmonise the wording of the two Acts, and **recommend** that there should be a liability on the Board to restore the property, works or land, as far as practicable, to its pre-damaged condition.

Repairing Subsidence Damage

117. The Board normally arrange for repairs to be carried out by their own contractors to ensure that subsidence damage is put right as far as is reasonable. In certain circumstances the Board choose to make a payment in lieu to enable claimants to make their own arrangements for repair, depending upon the Board's assessment of their own capacity to handle the repairs, as well as claimants' willingness to accept a payment. We consider this to be an unsatisfactory arrangement. We **recommend** that claimants should have the right to choose between repairs carried out by the Board and payments to contractors of their own choice so as to enable claimants to manage their own repairs. The right to choose by whom, and by what means, repairs to damaged property and land should be carried out is fundamental. It would not remove the right of a claimant to request the Board to arrange for the repairs to be carried out. But it would help the claimant who exercises the right to a payment to feel in charge of the repair of the property and, as a corollary, no longer in the hands of those whose activities had caused the damage in the first place. We would not expect the choice in practice to be exercised in a capricious way, but to reflect in time a balance between the personal circumstances of the claimant and the ability of the Board to procure

effective and efficient repairs. The balance will therefore be determined in part by the willingness of the Board to adapt their present practices in line with the recommendations we make in this chapter.

118.   The Board should be safeguarded against unreasonably high charges from a claimant or his chosen contractor. We **recommend** that costs should be settled in advance on the basis of an agreed schedule of repairs, with variations only admissible if additional work or other genuine difficulties arise. Disputes should be referred to independent adjudication. A schedule of repairs agreed with the claimant would remove any doubt or uncertainty over the extent of subsidence damage, enable stage payments to be made, and act as the basis for compensation in relation to each claim. It would provide a checklist against which repairs are actually carried out, and be the basis of a final inspection. It would also provide an accurate record of damage at the point of settlement of a claim: further damage would be the subject of a new schedule. In the event of a query from a prospective purchaser, there would be a full record of damage upon which a settlement had been reached.

119.   Delays in completing repairs, and poor standards of workmanship, can frequently be attributed to lack of effective supervision. An agreed schedule of repairs provides the basis for improved supervision. Where claimants opt to arrange for their own contractors, they of course take on the responsibility for ensuring that the work is carried out to their satisfaction, and they accept the contractual risks. In practice we would expect this responsibility to be exercised by specialist advisers acting on the claimant's behalf, who would see the contract through to final inspection. Where claimants opt to leave the arrangements to the Board, we **recommend** that the Board appoint a managing agent of their own to ensure that repairs are completed against the schedule to a proper standard and on time. Too often we have come across instances where supervision has been lax or non-existent. We understand that effective supervision imposes a burden on the Board, and that where manpower is thinly spread they may be tempted to leave the contractor to get on with the job. The level of supervision however provides a key measure of the importance the Board attach to putting damage right quickly and at least inconvenience to the claimant. We **recommend** that where necessary the Board consider augmenting their own resources by engaging outside professional advisers to act as their managing agents for this work. These agents would assist in the preparation and costing of schedules, their agreement with claimants, the supervision of contractors undertaking repairs, and handling queries that arise on contractual matters. We understand that the Board have employed outside quantity surveyors on an experimental basis to help in drawing up standard repair schedules, and our recommendation builds on this experience. We also **recommend** that in cases where severe subsidence damage is concentrated in particular locations the Board should similarly consider employing outside assistance to supplement their own resources, and ensure that supervision is exercised on-site. The presence of a representative of the Board in such circumstances would be widely welcomed by those affected and provide effective liaison between the Board and the local community. The representative would also be in a good position to judge whether the social or health services were required to assist a particular family or individual.

120.   Effective supervision of repair contracts should include in every case a final inspection. Once repairs are completed, as detailed in the schedule, we **recommend** that a final inspection is carried out and certified by a qualified surveyor independent of the Board (normally the claimant's agent), and countersigned by the claimant or their representative. This is normal commercial practice, but as far as we are aware it does not feature in the Board's current management procedures.

121.   Where the Board have assumed the responsibility for the repair of a number of properties in an area we see no objection to their current practice of using local contractors to carry out repairs, with the supply of standard materials provided under term contracts. Such contracts enable the Board to negotiate favourable rates for the work, and, providing adequate quality control is imposed, there are clear benefits to the Board and to claimants. This is a decision for the Board to take in the light of its contractual commitments in an area. Where they do so, however, we **recommend** that separate contracts are drawn up for the repair of individual properties against the agreed schedules, which should include provision for continuity of work and a contract completion time in all cases. These separate contracts should be drawn up, supervised, and finally inspected in the same way as any other contract entered into by the Board.

122.   We recognise that there are exceptional circumstances where it is clearly uneconomic or impracticable to repair a property because of the nature of the damage for which the Board is liable, and a compensation payment provides the only available remedy. Since the loss of the alternative remedy of repairs implies some curtailment of the choice available to claimants, we believe that the circumstances in which a compensation payment should be permissible need to be tightly defined. In particular, it is important to avoid a position whereby a claimant has insufficient resources either to carry out the necessary repairs or to move into a comparable property elsewhere. We **recommend** that the Board should be able to make compensation payments at market value instead of repairs only:

  (i)   where a claimant has a specific entitlement to compensation;
  (ii)   where full repairs are physically impossible – for example, where the structure of a badly tilted property is unsuited to jacking up;
  (iii)   where a property is so dilapidated as to make it impracticable to isolate or identify the mining subsidence damage;
  (iv)   where subsidence repairs are to be merged with other repairs or redevelopment, at the request of the claimant;
  (v)   where the cost of repairs exceeds by *at least 20%* the depreciation in the value of the property in its undamaged state.
  (vi)   where the Board, by agreement with the claimant, purchase the damaged property.

Where disputes arise, we **recommend** that independent adjudication should be available.

123. There are also circumstances where a property has been so severely damaged that the only realistic course of action is to demolish the property and either rebuild or pay compensation. It is particularly important that in such circumstances the decision to demolish is taken as quickly as possible, and in agreement with the claimant, and that any dispute is subject to adjudication. Where demolition is agreed the financial settlement should again be at market value, so that the claimant is able to purchase a similar property locally. Where this proves difficult, because there are no such houses available, we would expect the Board also to consider making a hardship payment to assist the claimant should he so wish. Where demolition has taken place it is important to avoid site dereliction, and where they continue to own the site the Board should take steps to ensure that it is secured and kept tidy until the land is sold or a new property is built. We would also expect the local planning authority to consider sympathetically any application for permission to build a replacement home.

Interim Repairs

124. We accept that, notwithstanding the widespread concern about the use of 'stop notices' under Section 3 of the 1957 Act, it is sensible to defer permanent repairs until there is a reasonable probability of ground movement ceasing. We find it difficult to understand why such a provision should be available only where claims are pursued under the 1957 Act, and **recommend** that this should be available to the Board in all circumstances where further ground movement is expected. This wider power carries with it a clear obligation on the Board to introduce strict conditions on the deployment and use of 'stop notices', and to ensure that these are renewed only where there is a clear justification for doing so. We **recommend** that 'stop notices' should lapse after one year, and, when served, should be accompanied by a clear explanation of the reasons for doing so, and of the rights of those upon whom they are served. They should not be renewed automatically, but be subject after one year to a critical review of their need and effects. Where they are renewed, a second letter should be sent explaining why this has been done, and indicating a timetable for the next steps leading to final repairs. It is essential that while a 'stop notice' is in force everything possible is done to ensure that the damage imposes as little inconvenience and discomfort as possible on the householder. Interim repairs should be carried out to a high standard, remedying any obviously unsightly effects, and ensuring that a household is able to live as comfortably as possible in the circumstances.

Temporary Accommodation

125. Where the damage to a house is so severe that it is unreasonable to expect the claimant to continue to live in the property until final repairs are carried out, or where a claimant has to be moved out whilst repairs are being executed, alternative accommodation may be provided by the Board. The Board seek to provide accommodation of a good standard which will be acceptable to the claimant. Where the claimant is anxious not to move far away from his home, a mobile home may be provided if a convenient site is available. When carried out sympathetically this is a sensible response by the Board to circumstances which are highly undesirable both for the family concerned and for the Board. We are not however persuaded that enough

imagination is always brought to bear on this problem where it occurs. Too often we have had brought to our attention cases where families have been put in houses patently unsuited to their needs, bearing in mind the length of time they are out of their own home, and their age and family structure.

126. It is important that a sufficient stock of houses is bought to provide an adequate choice for households who find, through no fault of their own, that they are displaced for long periods. We **recommend** that where a household is allocated temporary accommodation, an indication is given of the period for which this will be and that, as far as possible, a choice of alternative accommodation is given, perhaps including the possibility of a mobile home which can be sited near the vacated property. The accommodation offered should be of adequate size and standard in relation to the rehoused family, with all the necessities of a home, such as adequate heating, and in a well maintained condition. Full cooperation with the local housing authority is essential, especially in areas where damage is heavily concentrated, and we **recommend** that housing officers should play an active part wherever possible in resolving disputes about temporary accommodation between the Board and affected households.

127. Where families have left their homes, it is important that their property is treated with care and as far as possible in accordance with their wishes. Closer supervision of property temporarily vacated would help, and the Board should indicate that they are willing to discuss with claimants the possibility of their making their own arrangements for the security of their vacant property, on the understanding that the reasonable costs would be reimbursed by the Board.

Assistance to Claimants

128. People who wish to pursue claims against the Board often feel a need for specialist advice to help prepare their claim and deal with any differences of opinion with the Board before settlement. This is entirely understandable, and is often preferred by the Board in the more complex cases. The Board will normally contribute towards the fees of surveyors and other technical advisers for the purpose of preparing a claim and presenting this to the Board, except when the value of the settled claim does not exceed £250. We **recommend** the removal of this limit so that help with fees is available for any claimant who needs specialist advice regardless of the size of the claim.

129. Claimants should be free to employ whosoever appears to them qualified to provide the advice they need. We reject the notion that help should be confined to fees paid to an approved list of specialist advisers. There is some concern, however, about the availability of suitably qualified advisers in relation to mining subsidence claims. We share this concern. It is important that any scale of contributions agreed between the Board and the professions is set at a level which enables claimants to have reasonable access to good specialist advice. This is in the interests of both the Board and the claimant, and we **recommend** that the current scale of contributions is reviewed with this in mind. Where the Board make a contribution towards the fees of specialist advisers, we consider it also important that the amount paid should be clearly known to the claimant. We **recommend** that the Board

make all such contributions payable direct to the claimant who in turn will settle with the adviser.

130. We believe that these steps, together with the improvements we propose in relation to the submission of claims and the repair of damage, are also likely to be more effective in controlling the practices of agents and technical advisers operating in this field than any attempt to regulate directly their conduct by means of statute or a code of practice. No one profession represents the range of interests involved in mining subsidence claims, and there are therefore clear limits as to how far the codes traditionally used to regulate members of the established professional bodies could be usefully extended.

Land and Public Utilities

131. We have considered whether the greater emphasis on repair as against payment in lieu which we recommend in relation to domestic dwellings should also apply to land and infrastructure damaged by subsidence. Special arrangements already exist whereby the Board make payments to public utilities and to highway authorities so that these bodies can carry out repair works themselves, often as part of a more general scheme of improvement. We have no evidence to suggest that these arrangements are not working well. Similarly, in the case of the repair of industrial premises, the firm itself usually prefers to settle for a cash payment and put this towards a wider modernisation programme. This is sensible, and we see no reason to suggest any change in existing practice.

132. There is considerably more disquiet about the current balance between repair and compensation in so far as it relates to agricultural land damaged by subsidence. Evidence presented to us by the National Farmers' Union and by the Ministry of Agriculture, Fisheries and Food indicates that some Areas of the Board prefer increasingly to make payments instead of carrying out proper restoration. We have already emphasised the need for the Board to improve its prediction methods in agricultural areas, and to discuss appropriate preventive measures with farmers before mining takes place. It is equally important for damaged agricultural land to be fully restored to its pre-damaged condition in so far as this is practicable. Section 1(4)(i) of the 1957 Act requires the Board to consult the Ministry (in Scotland, the Secretary of State) before making any payments instead of restoration. The intention of this provision is clear: payments should be made only in exceptional circumstances. We **recommend** that the Board issue further guidance to their Areas drawing attention to the purpose of these provisions and ensuring that full and early consultation takes place with the Ministry of Agriculture, the Department of Agriculture and Fisheries in Scotland or the Welsh Office Agriculture Department in Wales, as appropriate, about the appropriate remedy for damaged agricultural land.

133. Similar considerations apply to both main and intermediate water-courses, whose efficiency has a vital effect on the condition of agricultural land. It is important that the Board consult water and drainage authorities at an early stage before mining takes place. Such consultation could be assured by appropriate representation on the Liaison Committees we have proposed

in the previous chapter. This should ensure that the necessary preventive measures are agreed and carried out. We also recommend that everything possible is done to put damage right, and that when legislation is consolidated as we propose in Chapter 9 the wording of Section 5 of the 1957 Act is reconsidered to limit the appropriate action to remedying or preventing any deterioration in the land drainage system.

CHAPTER 7

SCOPE OF COMPENSATION PROVISION

We consider in this chapter the extent to which the Board should further compensate households and public bodies, taking into account compensation practice elsewhere.

134. As explained in previous chapters the Board are required by the 1957 and 1975 Acts to make good, or pay compensation for, damage caused by subsidence. Broadly speaking, this applies only to land, buildings, structures or works, but the Board have long recognised that some other types of damage for which they have no legal liability may cause hardship to individuals. They have therefore since 1976 undertaken to give sympathetic consideration to such cases and to extend the range of items for which they are prepared to pay compensation.

135. The extent to which the Board go beyond their statutory obligations is described in detail in their own voluntary Code of Practice. This covers loss or damage to chattels (for example, plant and machinery, stocks of goods, livestock, household possessions), home loss payments, depreciation of crops, farm loss payments, and loss of value arising from tilt or other structural distortion. In cases of dispute over these issues the Board are prepared to go to independent adjudication. They are also willing to ensure that hardship is prevented by, for example, purchasing a damaged house at undamaged value if the owner has to sell, or providing alternative accommodation for small businesses. These measures were widely welcomed at the time of their introduction, and they continue to provide an important supplementary source of recompense to those affected by subsidence damage. The Board have indicated to us that these measures have contributed substantially to their overall costs of subsidence repair and compensation, although since in practice they do not distinguish between payments made under statute and under the Code we have not been able to verify this to our own satisfaction.

136. Despite these measures there has been continued criticism of the Code of Practice on two counts. First, that since it remains a voluntary Code, the Board can in theory withdraw it at any time, and the benefits which it confers are therefore intrinsically inferior to rights available under statute. Secondly, that its provisions fall short of what should be available to claimants in comparison with compensation for damage available elsewhere. Much of the institutional evidence to us has been along these lines. The view has previously been reflected in the two Private Members' Bills referred to in paragraph 40.

137. We identified five areas, not necessarily mutually exclusive of each other, where pressure to extend the scope of compensation provision beyond that currently available under statute and the Code has been evident: for incidental expenditure incurred during the process of claim and restitution; for stress and strain to individuals; for inconvenience and disturbance

resulting from damage, and in the course of repairs; for loss in property value; and for consequential loss. In examining these issues, and in seeking to identify whether sensible provision can be made for them, we have sought to balance the need to respond sympathetically to genuine cases of hardship with the probable costs and effectiveness of possible remedies, as well as the possible implications for other areas of compensation practice. We have also recognised that the Board have statutory or contractual rights to remove support from the surface, and these have to be weighed against the rights of the surface owner.

Incidental Costs

138.   In practice the Board reimburse claimants for those incidental costs which are seen to be directly attributable to the repair of the damage, although this is not clear from the wording of the present Code. Items of expenditure which are currently reimbursed include the repair or replacement of damaged furniture or carpets, telephone calls, travel expenses, cleaning, additional expenses incurred whilst living in alternative accommodation, and loss of earnings — provided reasonable steps are taken in each case to prevent or minimise this expenditure. As in the case of disturbance payments under the Land Compensation Act, these payments relate to items of expenditure which are capable of being readily assessed. We **recommend** that there should be statutory provision for compensation for those items of expenditure reasonably incurred in the effective pursuit of admitted claims. Where claims are not admitted, the Board should also consider making a discretionary payment to help genuine claimants. In the meantime we **recommend** that the information provided by the Board and by the Department of Energy make explicit the items of claim for which compensation is available, provided such expenses have been reasonably incurred, and that independent adjudication is available in case of dispute. This should also be brought to the claimant's attention early in the process of agreeing the basis of a claim.

Stress and Strain

139.   We have little doubt that subsidence damage, and the often lengthy process of securing effective repair and compensation for that damage, can cause considerable personal stress and strain. In the worst cases, it may impair the health of the more vulnerable members of the community. But stress and strain are not confined to those who suffer mining subsidence damage and, as far as we are aware, no special provision for compensation for this is available to those similarly affected by other public works. This is not in itself a definitive argument against such provision, but we believe that there are important reasons for not introducing it. First, any contributory subsidence damage results from a lawful activity on the part of the Board, and it would seem wrong to place them in a position different from that of any other public body. Secondly, it would be extremely difficult to assess the degree of strain and stress attributable to subsidence damage, and to define the circumstances in which compensation would be available. Thirdly, we strongly believe that there is considerable scope for reducing stress and strain by tackling the main causes at source — by avoiding or reducing damage in the first place, by adopting a more caring attitude in the carrying out and management of repairs, by providing better information about mining

44

intentions and indivdual rights to compensation, and by easier access to independent adjudication in the case of disputes. The Code of Practice provides some opportunity for the Board to exercise their discretion in favour of claimants who have been subject to inordinate stress and strain, and the Board have indicated that they will continue to make "hardship" payments wherever these would help to minimise evident distress. In the light of these considerations, we concur with the view taken by the Commission on Energy and the Environment that stress and strain to individuals is best dealt with by improving the process of repairs and the settlement of claims, together with an imaginative and compassionate operation of the Code of Practice and associated hardship payments.

Inconvenience and Disturbance

140. Similar arguments have been advanced against the provision of compensation for the serious inconvenience and disturbance occasionally experienced when the repair of subsidence damage is long drawn out and where there is an identifiable loss of home amenity. Here again we are of the view that the proper and speedy execution of repairs, together with sympathetic operation of the Code of Practice, can reduce the incidence and severity of inconvenience and disturbance in many instances. Nevertheless we have been forcibly struck by the special combination of circumstances associated with mining subsidence damage that can give rise to a family living in substandard conditions where internal structural damage has been serious and where repairs are long drawn out. This may be due to the extent of damage or to the deferment of repairs at the insistence of the Board (for example, where a 'stop notice' is served), and where suitable accommodation is not available elsewhere. In these circumstances, family and home life can be seriously disrupted for long periods without provision for compensation for disturbance. We understand that in practice the Board in some Areas react sympathetically by eventually carrying out more extensive repairs and, in some cases, by making discretionary payments. In our view this merely highlights the existence of a significant problem, and accentuates the fact that there is at present no effective remedy. We do not believe this to be right. We are firmly of the view that recognition of the need for compensation in all such circumstances would confirm the Board's commitment to alleviate hardship caused by subsidence damage, and would meet a genuine concern of those affected in the way we have described.

141. We have considered three broad options. First, the Board might make discretionary hardship payments in recognition of the exceptional inconvenience and disturbance suffered by a small minority of claimants. In this case it would be left to the Board to determine where and when it would be appropriate to make a payment, and what amount to pay. This is the current position, at least in some Areas. Secondly, the present head of claim for home loss in the Code of Practice might be extended to include provision for households remaining in their home under exceptionally trying conditions. Home loss payments are however modelled on provisions in the Land Compensation Act and as such are tied to a permanent move from the property. They are also based on rateable values. In our view it would be inappropriate to use this formula as there would seem to be no valid link between rateable value and the sort of hardship we have identified. Indeed it

could be argued that there is an inverse relationship. The third option is a new head of claim which would be confined to the sort of circumstances outlined in the previous paragraph, with provision for payments primarily related to the duration and severity of the inconvenience and disturbance.

142. Our intention is to ensure that those who experience an exceptional degree of inconvenience and disturbance, amounting in effect to a loss of home amenity, should be suitably compensated. We therefore **recommend** that a new head of claim for loss of home amenity should be part of a revised Code of Practice, available to those households who have suffered from a long period of inconvenience and disturbance in their own home as a result of subsidence damage and subsequent repair, and should be paid as a lump sum to the claimant once repairs have finally been completed. The amount should be linked to the scale and duration of damage, and should reflect matters not covered by other items of claim. We believe that the existence of such a head of claim in a revised Code of Practice would make a substantial contribution to meeting a real identifiable need, and have a positive impact on the Board's image in mining areas.

Loss in Property Values

143. We have received evidence from a wide range of sources suggesting that the Board should pay compensation for loss in property values both in advance of mining taking place and following subsidence damage.

144. Property values can certainly fall in advance of mining taking place, and in expectation of subsidence damage occuring, in spite of the Board's legal obligations to make restitution for that damage. Property values in a coal-mining area can also fall for a wide variety of reasons totally unrelated to mining activity. In many circumstances, whatever the reason for a fall, property values will recover in due course and the loss will be accepted as temporary only. This cyclical effect has been evident in those areas where future coal mining activity has achieved considerable publicity — through public inquiries for example — and where most of the pressure to provide compensation has originated. As new coal fields are opened up in areas hitherto untouched by mining, similar pressures are likely to arise from communities unfamiliar with such industrial development. We have been conscious of the possible financial consequences for both the coal industry and other major industrial undertakings of any recommendations we make on loss of property value.

145. Provisions in the Town and Country Planning Act 1971 require a public authority to acquire property where it is likely to be compulsorily purchased and cannot as a result be sold at a reasonable price. Where the property is not liable to be compulsorily purchased there is no provision to require the authority to buy it, even though the prospect of public works on neighbouring land may reduce the current market value of the property. Nor is there any provision for compensation for such a loss of value, since the acquisition of a property does not carry with it the right to a particular environmental amenity. We agree with the Commission on Energy and the Environment that in this respect coal mining is no different from other forms of public development, and to require the Board to compensate for a loss in property

value arising from the expectation of subsidence damage would not be justified.

146. We were asked to consider specifically whether compensation should be paid to the owner of a property, the value of which had fallen as a result of subsidence damage even though repairs had been carried out by the Board. The Commission on Energy and the Environment argued that there was a case on grounds of equity for such compensation if a house were left with a tilt or obvious repair to an unsightly crack which made it less attractive than its neighbours. They further argued that the Board implicitly recognised this by making discretionary cash payments in certain cases in addition to carrying out repairs. The Board subsequently agreed to extend their code of Practice to cover residual loss arising from unremedied damage, defined as tilt or similar structural distortion, but not from remedied damage. Loss of value is currently calculated at the point when repairs to the property have been completed.

147. We agree with the Commission that if there is a material loss of value following completion of repairs then compensation should be payable to the owner of the property. In the vast majority of cases the amount and quality of repairs will be such as to produce no discernible loss of value at all. Our concern is to ensure as far as is practicable that where permanent loss in value occurs, compensation is determined on the basis of a clearly identifiable material and physical change in the condition of the property such as results, for example, from the substantial rebuilding of the side of a house. We **recommend** that the provision currently made for compensation for structural distortion is widened accordingly, and given statutory backing.

148. The Board currently consider the purchase of a property when it cannot be sold because it has been damaged by mining subsidence or, in exceptional cases, because it is in imminent danger of damage from advancing workings. The decision to purchase is taken against two broad criteria: (a) whether hardship is being caused by the failure to sell the property on the open market, and (b) whether mining subsidence damage is the reason why the property cannot be sold. They define hardship to include cases where an owner has to sell because he or she has obtained another job outside reasonable daily travelling distance, because financial or family circumstances have so materially altered — for example through redundancy, retirement or children leaving home — that the household must move to less expensive accommodation, or because illness or incapacity necessitates a move to a different type of property. In addition, the Board usually require every reasonable effort to have been made to sell on the open market at a reasonable asking price, by proper advertising and the employment of an agent, and the property must have been offered for sale for at least three months. The price paid by the Board would normally be based on the value of similar property in the locality which is undamaged and unaffected by the threat of damage. The vendor's costs are not normally paid. The Board will also consider, in similar circumstances, making a top-up payment to an owner whose house is sold at the best price that could be obtained at the time but which is lower than the undamaged market value of the property. A copy of the conveyance or transfer to the purchaser must be obtained as evidence that

may be taken into account if a further claim is made later in respect of that property. In both these cases, the decision whether to purchase or compensate for loss on a forced sale is at the discretion of the Board, and adjudication is not available.

149. We appreciate the Board's aim to avoid a major excursion into the domestic property market, where sale prospects vary widely through time and in different localities. We consider the Board's policy towards house purchase and compensation wholly reasonable in the circumstances. We nonetheless **recommend** that specific publicity should be given in the Code to the circumstances in which they will purchase and that independent adjudication should be available in case of disputes about both the decision to purchase, and the financial settlement. We do not consider that there is a case for extending the current criteria further: in our view they strike the right balance between the Board's interests and those of affected households, as long as they continue to be applied sympathetically in all the Board's Areas.

150. Occasionally the Board purchase a property because a building society has been unwilling to lend money to a prospective purchaser of a damaged house. In some cases the Board are able to give advice to the building society which results in a mortage being granted, but some reluctance on the part of the building societies, particularly in new mining areas, is of concern. We welcome the Board's willingness to discuss with the building societies the possibility of an arrangement whereby the Board might underwrite any prospective loss to a building society resulting from the effects of subsidence where there is an undischarged claim. We **recommend** that such discussions are initiated as soon as possible.

Consequential Loss

151. We have considered these specific areas of possible compensation having regard to the evidence of genuine hardship amongst those affected by subsidence damage, and to the costs their amelioration would impose on the Board. Nonetheless considerable support has been expressed for the view that there should be a general right to compensation for all consequential, as well as direct, losses arising from subsidence damage. Such consequential losses as we understand them, would include, in so far as they affect individuals, some of the incidental costs, property value losses, and stress, strain and inconvenience on which we have made recommendations. Similarly, consequential losses to an enterprise might include loss of business profits, orders, or contracts, and to a local authority or other public body, loss of revenue from reduced rates or rents, or increased maintenance costs.

152. Statutory undertakers are generally required to pay compensation for damage caused by the exercise of their functions, although, as far as we are aware, this stops short of a liability to meet all consequential losses, tangible and intangible. The approach of the courts has nonetheless been to treat claims as if the compensation were damages for legalised tort, and to deal accordingly with the question of whether particular losses are too remote to be admissible for compensation. In effect, this means that no general rule can be applied, and it is a matter of judgement how far it is reasonable for the Board to go in meeting such claims. Surface owners clearly have some

responsibility to take steps to minimise the likelihood of damage and of losses, except where their title otherwise provides. We take the view that although it is right to adjust the current balance further in favour of the surface owner, it would not be reasonable to make the Board fully responsible for all consequential losses. This places on the Board a special responsibility to adopt a caring and sympathetic attitude to those affected by subsidence damage, and we have sought to reflect this in the recommendations we have made.

153.   In the case of commercial or industrial undertakings, compensation is already available under the Code of Practice for damages to stock in trade, plant and machinery. The main outstanding question is whether compensation should also be paid for loss of business profits, contracts and orders where their activities are disrupted by subsidence damage. In practice the Board work closely with such enterprises to help minimise damage and to avoid losses. We consider that the present arrangements strike the right balance between the Board and the surface owner, providing a sufficient incentive for both to ensure that damage is kept to a minimum. We nevertheless **recommend** that the Board should make special efforts in the case of small enterprises, and consider making a hardship payment where it is clear that the enterprise has little flexibility to adjust its working arrangements and substantial personal losses have been incurred.

154.   Compensation available to agricultural enterprises is already wider in scope than that available to industry. This is justified in terms of the close relationship that exists between most types of agricultural production and the condition of the land itself, and of the difficulty in changing farming practices so as to limit the effect of damage. Farmers are therefore also able to obtain compensation for loss of crops, payable each year so long as the land remains affected by subsidence damage. Where land is made incapable of further beneficial use, then compensation is available to the owner for the full former value of the land, and to the tenant as a disturbance payment. Farm loss payments are also available where the farmer has to move to another farm. We have received evidence to suggest that these special arrangements, whilst generous, do not go far enough in recognising the effect a permanent loss or deterioration of land might have on the farm unit as a whole, as for example when damage to land results in an enforced, if gradual, shift towards lower value crops and in additional investment required to support the new use. We **recommend** that compensation should be available not only for the value of land taken permanently out of a holding but also for the diminution in value of the balance of that holding, providing this can be demonstrated. This would place the Board in a similar position to that of an acquiring authority which takes farmland by compulsory purchase.

155.   The most difficult area is in relation to the activities of public utilities where, for example, the escape of water from a fractured main can cause considerable damage to neighbouring properties or land. We understand that the Board are reluctant to accept responsibility for this sort of consequential loss: public utilities, particularly the water authorities, appear also reluctant to do so. Under Section 6 of the Water Act 1981 water undertakings are liable, with certain exceptions, for loss or damage arising as a result of an

escape of water from a main or communication pipe. The main exception is where the injured party has been partly or wholly responsible for the escape. Responsibility for meeting these sorts of loss would seem to rest in the first instance with the undertaking, and there would seem no good reason for their delaying payment to an injured party. This does not prevent the undertaking from pursuing subsequently a claim against the Board if they consider the original damage to have been caused by subsidence. This seems to us right in principle, and we do not consider that the Board's general liability should be extended to cover such consequential losses.

156.   Local authorities and other public bodies have also suggested that the Board should pay a contribution towards any additional maintenance or running costs incurred by public authorities following repair. We understand that this is already done in relation to some utilities, where compensation includes a commuted sum for subsequent higher maintenance costs. We believe that this is again right in principle, and that any settlement should include such provision. The method of settlement is best left to the parties concerned, although we would favour a lump sum payment (to include a commuted sum for ongoing costs) which would in effect discharge the Board's liabilities.

CHAPTER 8

RESOLVING DISPUTES

We explore in this chapter the way in which appropriate provision can be made for resolving disputes between the Board and claimants, and for financial assistance to the small claimant.

157. Disputes between the Board and individual claimants are inevitable under a system dealing with many thousands of claims each year. Differences of opinion can arise across a wide front, including the extent to which damage is attributable to coal mining subsidence, the extent of the Board's liability, the amount and kind of compensation payable, and the standard of repairs. Some of our witnesses mistakenly believed that there was no provision at all for appeal and arbitration. Others contended that the available means of challenging decisions of the Board were unsuitable or ineffective, and that a new appellate body should be created to adjudicate in mining subsidence disputes. Almost all stressed the need for a relatively informal and accessible means whereby disputes could be resolved quickly and inexpensively.

Existing Provisions

158. The statutory avenues of appeal to the Courts or to the Lands Tribunals in England, Wales and Scotland are outlined in paragraph 31 and the Board's commitment to arbitration to settle disputes arising under the Code of Practice in paragraph 37. We have found, however, that these procedures are little used. Few cases — mainly larger claims — have gone to arbitration or appeal, with the result that the efficacy of the existing provisions has not really been tested in respect of the sort of subsidence damage claims with which we are particularly concerned. Amongst the reasons cited in evidence for the reluctance to use these procedures was the very real fear of incurring heavy costs; ignorance of their existence; an apparent lack of encouragement by officials of the Board or by professional advisers; and a widespread belief that the courts and tribunals were invariably slow, remote, formal and generally intimidating to those who sought to argue their case against a powerful body like the National Coal Board.

159. This general ignorance of appeal rights is not altogether surprising, since the Board's publications about the compensation scheme, and their claim forms, make no mention of them. The booklet on the Code of Practice states that disputes may be settled by arbitration, but it contains no advice on the ways in which a claimant can proceed further. We have also seen letters sent by the Board rejecting claims without a satisfactory reason for doing so and without any mention of the possibility of an appeal if claimants are dissatisfied. We consider it imperative that claimants should be told in writing, wherever appropriate, of their rights in relation to adjudication. We **recommend** that the National Coal Board and the Department of Energy revise their relevant booklets, leaflets and forms to include full information on this subject. Letters sent by the Board rejecting claims should also refer to claimants' rights to adjudication, and the Board should encourage their

officials as a matter of course to remind people of their rights to independent adjudication, and to help them pursue this route if they so wish.

A New Appeal Body?

160.   We have given careful consideration to the proposal to create an entirely new appeal body. Some of those who advocated such a body were conscious of the attendant difficulties in adding to the number of tribunals or other appellate bodies. We were particularly conscious of the evident scarcity of skills — both technical and administrative — that would be needed, and the costs involved in setting up an entirely new body. These fears were confirmed in discussion with the Council on Tribunals and the Lands Tribunal. It also seemed to us that the County Court and Sheriff Court, with their high volume and great diversity of business, were less well placed than the Lands Tribunal to take on the burden of mining subsidence appeals. In the absence of convincing evidence that the potential of existing provisions had been fully explored, our initial view was that it would be difficult to justify a new tribunal at the present time.

161.   The Lands Tribunal includes amongst its members both lawyers and surveyors, and appears in principle well suited to the kind of specialist appeals which arise in relation to mining subsidence. They also command the support of the Board. We asked the Tribunal for England and Wales about the content and the weight of cases with which they normally dealt, the degree of formality at their hearings and the time taken, on average, to determine appeals. They assured us that they were well used to dealing with small cases, often involving a single dwelling, in the field of compulsory purchase and rating appeals. Hearings in such cases could be arranged locally and were usually quite informal, and the delays of past years had been eliminated so that cases could be heard within a few weeks if necessary. At the Tribunal's invitation, some of our members attended as observers at several hearings in London and Sheffield. They were impressed on each occasion by the trouble taken to put appellants at their ease as far as possible, and to assist each of them to present his or her own case to the best of their ability. The Tribunal also expressed their readiness and capacity to take on the additional work likely to result from proper communication to mining subsidence sufferers of their right of appeal against decisions of the Board.

162.   In the light of this, and of the established position of the Tribunal as an expert appeal body under existing legislation, we conclude that the Lands Tribunal remains the most appropriate body to consider appeals on mining subsidence damage. But in view of the small number of such cases historically dealt with by the Tribunal, we **recommend** that their procedures are examined so as to ensure that everything possible is being done to meet the needs of the small claimant in dispute with the Board and, three years after the new arrangements we propose come into effect, that their membership and practices are reviewed. In the meantime, the Board, the Department of Energy, and the Tribunal itself, should give greater publicity to the Tribunal's role in disputes of this kind.

163.   Although we reject the idea of a wholly new appellate body, we are very firmly of the view that for the large majority of straightforward minor

cases generated by the subsidence compensation system an appeal to the Lands Tribunal is likely to be both inappropriate and uneconomic. We **recommend** that claimants in dispute with the Board should have the choice of determination either by reference to an independent adjudicator selected according to their particular skills and impartiality from a regional list, or by reference to the Tribunal. Referral to independent adjudication should be by agreement between the claimant and the Board, whose consent should not be unreasonably withheld. In substitution for the arrangements under the present Code, claimants who opt for determination in this way should have no further right of appeal from the adjudicator's decision, save on a point of law, as this would negate the main purpose of establishing a quick and satisfactory settlement procedure at local level and at a reasonable cost. The adjudicator should be able to refer a case to the Tribunal if he considers this body more appropriate to decide the issue, whether it be on a point of fact or of law.

164.   We therefore **recommend** that a list of adjudicators on subsidence disputes be established. The Department of Energy should take the lead in inviting bodies such as the Royal Institution of Chartered Surveyors and the Law Society to nominate members for each coalfield area. The lists should be made widely available throughout coalfield areas, and should be revised regularly.

Contributions to Claimants' Costs

165.   We have previously made the point that the costs of an appeal against a decision of the Board loom large in deterring claimants who consider they may have a grievance. Although legal aid is available for cases brought to the Lands Tribunal by those who qualify for help under the national Legal Aid Scheme, generally speaking only claimants of very modest means are likely to qualify. Awards of costs by the Lands Tribunal usually follow the event — that is to say, if appellants succeed their costs will be paid by the Board; if the appeal fails they will be called on to pay the Board's costs as well as their own. In this matter mining subsidence appellants are treated no differently from other appellants — for example, those who choose to contest before the Tribunal the compensation offered them for property lost to a motorway or other public development. As a general rule, we see no good reason for distinguishing the Board's responsibility in cases of appeal from that of others in this position. But we feel sufficient concern for small claimants with a good *prima facie* case to prompt some special consideration on their behalf. Our objective has been to protect their interests without encouraging automatic free appeal against the Board's decisions or appeals that are frivolous or unreasonable.

166.   We understand that in some circumstances when officers conducting small cases heard by the Lands Tribunal in other areas of dispute are asked if they intend to seek costs if they are successful, they name only a nominal sum. This line is often taken to assist claimants acting in person, always provided that they are not held by the Tribunal to have acted unreasonably in bringing the matter to appeal. A policy of this kind commends itself to the Committee as a means of limiting the element of risk for appellants, and of enabling them to assess their position more positively when they have to decide whether to pursue a case to appeal. It does not answer all the demands expressed to us on

their behalf but we **recommend** that the Board should consider as a matter of policy offering at least this measure of help with costs on Lands Tribunal cases.

167.   Prudent would-be appellants will seek professional help in the first instance to discover whether they have a *prima facie* case (this is, in any case, a prerequisite for the receipt of legal aid). Discussions are currently taking place between the RICS and the Citizens' Advice Bureaux to extend the Chartered Surveyors' Voluntary Service to include mining subsidence damage, and if agreement is reached appellants may be able to obtain free help from this source. We understand that the Citizens' Advice Bureaux will then advise whether there is such a service in a particular area. The Lands Tribunal also told us that they do their best to advise people who approach them on the jurisdiction of the Tribunal and the type of evidence that would be needed to present a case to them.

168.   In the case of a dispute settled by independent adjudication we would not expect the costs incurred by either party to be very large, since by the time a decision is taken to use this form of determination both sides will have prepared their case, usually through the exchange of correspondence, and claimants would not normally require additional professional advice. We therefore take the view that the parties should meet their own costs, with the fees of the adjudicator met by the Board.

CHAPTER 9

THE FRAMEWORK OF CONTROL, MANAGEMENT AND MONITORING

In this chapter we indicate the framework of control which we consider necessary to underpin the compensation scheme over future years. We also consider parallel improvements to the management of the scheme and the monitoring of its administration.

The Framework of Control

169. Some of the shortcomings of the compensation scheme can be remedied only by changes in the framework of current legislation and controls. We have sought to identify these changes and to indicate the form they might take in earlier chapters. They are designed to strengthen the main thrust of existing statute rather than provide a wholly new emphasis. Nonetheless, the two main pieces of existing legislation, although broadly similar in intent, contain subtle differences of emphasis which serve to confuse rather than elucidate the rights of claimants and the Board — and which make the management and administration of the scheme more difficult than it need be.

170. On balance we believe that some consolidation of these provisions is needed. We **recommend** the consolidation and extension of the 1957 and 1975 Acts to ensure that the main statutory underpinning of the compensation scheme is clear to all as to both scope and intent. It should emphasise the Board's prime responsibility to repair or put right subsidence damage, and should provide a statutory right to compensation for the heads of claim currently available under the present Code of Practice. The Code's provisions were couched from the beginning in specific terms so that they could be taken into statute as and when necessary. We believe that this should now be done as part of a consolidation exercise, which might also have regard to the special agreements negotiated between the Board and a number of statutory undertakings. Many of the details of the new statutory framework, particularly those associated with the 1957 Act and the Code, could with benefit be brought together in associated secondary legislation. We would also envisage a place for a new Code of Practice incorporating the main discretionary elements of the system. Such a Code might include for example the areas of provision currently covered by hardship payments, as well as our proposals for loss of home amenity, for house purchase, and for some aspects of notification. This would be compatible with other Codes of Practice where flexibility is important.

171. We recognise that it will be difficult to adjust the framework of control in this way very quickly. We do not, however, consider it possible to amend piecemeal the existing body of statute without adding to the present confusion about its scope and intent. Many of our proposals can however be put into effect by administrative action, particularly through additions and modifications to the Code of Practice, and we see some benefit in this in the short term provided it is accompanied by a clear commitment to consolidate the main

55

legislative provisions without delay. We would have very serious misgivings about any attempt to rely on a revised Code alone as a means of meeting fully our proposals to improve the framework of control.

172.   Other shortcomings in the present system — including unacceptable variations in practice between Areas, and poor communications within the Board and between the Board and the public — can be explained by inadequacies in administration and failures in management. Until these are put right it will be difficult to realise the full benefits of the changes we have recommended. We understand that the Board are at present reviewing the way in which the compensation scheme is administered, and we therefore consider it timely to make our own suggestions for improvements.

173.   The Commission on Energy and the Environment took the view that there was a need for a sustained and coherent lead from Board Headquarters on environmental policy, and on the means whereby such policy be effected locally. We strongly concur with this in relation to subsidence. The advantages claimed for the present system — that it allows the exercise of discretion in the field and the sympathetic treatment of individual hardship — appear often to be experienced by claimants as unexplained inconsistencies in the interpretation of the provisions on which they rely for relief. We accept the need for flexibility in administering the system at Area level, but consider that a more effective system of overall management and control is now required. This would ensure that current best practice is applied more widely, and costs are contained.

A Separate Commission?

174.   A number of those who have given evidence have suggested that the responsibility for administering the compensation scheme and making restitution should be removed from the Board and vested in a new commission set up by Government. Amongst advocates of this change, Jack Ashley CH MP introduced a Bill into Parliament under the Ten Minute Rule in February 1979. The main arguments in its favour are that much of the complaint and resentment which has led to the current review arises from the position of the Board, which causes the subsidence damage in the first instance and then often appears to determine liability and payment in an arbitrary fashion, and from an advantageous position. This was a common complaint and may explain the sense of helplessness expressed in the evidence of many witnesses and in the replies given by informants in the independent survey. Those who advocate the setting up of a separate commission argue that an independent body is better able to hold an even balance between the resources of a great nationalised industry and those at the other extreme, for example individual owner-occupiers or tenants.

175.   After careful consideration we reject this proposal. Transfer of the administration of the compensation scheme to a separate commission would dilute the Board's responsibility and would reduce the incentive that exists to adopt the precautionary and preventive measures to minimise subsidence damage discussed in Chapter 4. It would introduce a third party between the Board and the claimants, and tend to increase the isolation of the two parties which we have already exposed. It would inhibit the Board's responsibility to

pay more attention to the effect of mining subsidence on the environment, and to see that the public are better informed of their activities. Finally, the administrative cost of a separate commission would be high and require additional expertise and manpower. For all these reasons, we consider that a commission would be unable to realise to the full the benefit we believe can be obtained through proper implementation of our recommendations.

Management Practice

176.   We consider that the improvements in administration that we are seeking are best achieved through a system of management self-regulation on the part of the Board. Such self-regulation is established and effective in several industries where the main board of a company or group wishes to ensure that its policies are effectively implemented by its subsidiary companies or divisions. The principle of self-regulation is compatible with the Board's present organisation structure operating through Area management, with guidance on implementation of policy from the main Board. The improvements we suggest to the management system could be introduced at little or no additional cost.

177.   As a first step we **recommend** that the Board should publish a statement in general terms outlining their policies on compensation for subsidence damage. As a minimum we suggest that such a statement should include:

(a)   recognition by the Board that their mining activities may have an adverse effect on the surface environment and cause damage to buildings and property, and a declaration of the Board's policy to mitigate these adverse effects by using the best practical means, consistent with their obligation to extract coal efficiently and economically;

(b)   a statement that the Board's policy is to comply with their legal obligations to compensate those who have suffered damage from subsidence, and to apply the terms of their Code of Practice. The Board might also state that they will use their best endeavours to deal with claims for compensation expeditiously and sympathetically so as to mitigate hardship to property owners, tenants and members of the general public;

(c)   commitment to provide all information necessary to give prior warning to those who may be affected by mining activities and to notify them of their rights to compensation for damage arising from subsidence, and how a claim may be made for restitution and repair of the loss and damage caused;

(d)   recognition that there is a need to develop and maintain public confidence in the Board's commitment to carry out their mining activities with proper regard for the public interest, through consultation with local authorities, statutory undertakings and, where appropriate, members of the general public.

178.   A policy statement of this sort on subsidence compensation would provide the framework within which detailed guidance could be prepared for

Area management and for the Board's officers in the field. This guidance, perhaps in the form of a procedures manual, could indicate for example how claims submitted under a revised Code of Practice should be treated, and in what circumstances the Board would consider making hardship payments. This would, essentially, be an extension of the present practice of providing occasional guidance notes to Areas.

179.   We also **recommend** that the Board should set up management audit review teams, staffed with the appropriate level of expertise, to monitor the performance of Areas in dealing with compensation claims. It is essential that the audit teams should be independent of Area management and should have the authority to carry out a thorough investigation, and that they should report directly to a main Board Member. The audit team should draw attention to inadequacies and inconsistencies in the management of the compensation system and make recommendations for remedial action.

180.   We were surprised to find no publicly available statement explaining the costs incurred in meeting subsidence claims and the way in which the compensation scheme operates. The Board's Annual Report for 1982/83, for example, merely gives the total costs incurred by surface damage (including the reclamation of opencast sites), records that this Committee has been established and notes that a further head of claim has been added to the Code of Practice in the last year. We believe the absence of a fuller public statement on subsidence to be unfortunate. Greater willingness to account publicly for the operation of the scheme would promote better understanding of the consequences of higher subsidence damage costs, and provide an incentive for the Board to demonstrate the efficacy of their policies and practice. We **recommend** that the Board should report annually to the Secretary of State for Energy on the administration of the compensation scheme. The report should be published and laid before Parliament. It should explain changes in the pattern of expenditure from the previous year, specify where shortcomings have been identified, and indicate what action has been taken or is proposed to rectify them.

Management Information and Staff Resources

181.   It is for the Board in the first instance to decide what information they need in order to achieve effective monitoring of costs and performance. We have been disturbed by the lack of information on the operation of the scheme readily available to the Board, and by the apparently haphazard choice of data collected at Area level. We received no convincing explanation of recent trends in the number and pattern of claims, and in the costs attributable to subsidence repair and compensation. We have seen no indication that the necessary analysis of such trends has been commissioned on a regular basis, although we understand that the Board intend to computerise more of such information in response to the rising costs of remedying subsidence damage. We view this apparent failure to analyse such trends, and to explain them convincingly, with considerable concern, and **recommend** that the Board should carry out a more systematic appraisal of the pattern of subsidence claims and costs, and relate this, wherever possible, to their mining operations. We also **recommend** that the Board should review urgently the information that they will require at Headquarters and Area

level in the light of our proposals for the management of the compensation scheme, in order to secure adequate control over expenditure and to monitor performance effectively. The review should cover all types of claim, 'stop notices', payments made under the various heads in the Code of Practice, and hardship payments.

182.   Similarly it is for the Board to decide on the level and distribution of staff resources required to administer the compensation scheme. We noted in Chapter 3 that in the year for which figures were available there was no apparent match of staff resources and the number of claims handled in the different Areas. Although this mismatch may be exceptional, we formed the impression that there was a good deal of inflexibility in the use of scarce manpower, and that the Board were unable to respond as quickly as they might both to the changing pattern of claims received and to the incidence of damage expected to result from taking out a particular panel of coal. We have suggested elsewhere in our report that in some cases the Board should consider the employment of outside specialists to supplement their own resources, and in the case of severe damage occurring to a particular locality, should seek the assistance of local authorities in harnessing all the necessary skills to help alleviate hardship. We also **recommend** that the Board should introduce more flexibility in the deployment of their own staff to meet the fluctuating workload implied by changes in mining activity and in the incidence of damage.

183.   We place great weight on these improved management practices. They could in themselves bring about a considerable improvement in the handling of compensation claims, even without the changes in legislation which we recommend. They are in any case essential if money is to be spent effectively and if expenditure is to be properly controlled. Set alongside the greater efforts which we consider the Board should make to publicise what they are doing — and often doing well — these changes would in due course transform the image and substance of the subsidence compensation scheme to the benefit of both the Board and the public.

Meeting the Costs

184.   In formulating our ideas and formal recommendations we have been alert to the possible costs these might impose both on the Board and on the public purse. We have sought to consider the benefits that we would expect to accrue against the cost to the Board. In a number of cases we have sought guidance from the Board as to the broad extent of costs implied by various specific measures, and against different assumptions. This invariably proved most difficult. It reinforces our view that there is an urgent need for better cost information on subsidence in order to provide an agreed starting point for assessing new proposals and options. In the absence of this, any such assessment must remain highly speculative.

185.   We recognise that a number of our proposals may help to add to what is already a considerable financial sum paid out under the existing compensation scheme. Nevertheless these costs form part of the true price of winning coal. In order therefore to maintain public confidence in the industry, and thus to ensure general acceptance of new production capacity,

they should be viewed as key items in the bill the nation must expect to pay for the retention of a secure domestic supply of coal. There is much scope for containing costs providing the scheme is managed and administered efficiently and effectively, but the level of costs is already such that the Board will increasingly need to question whether the need for coal outweighs the subsidence costs incurred, and whether the remedy lies more in prevention than in repair and compensation after damage has occurred. We believe that our recommendations provide the right balance between the need for coal and the protection of those who stand to be affected by the mining operations this need implies.

CHAPTER 10

GUIDE TO THE PRINCIPAL RECOMMENDATIONS

In this chapter we bring together the substance of our principal recommendations. Each is cross-referenced to the appropriate paragraph in the main body of our report, which gives the precise terms of the recommendation and sets it in its proper context.

Prediction and Prevention

186. *Prediction*

   i. The Board should carry out detailed geological surveys where there is evidence that ground movement is likely to be appreciable. (Para 78)

   ii. The British Geological Survey should investigate the reliability of the published geological maps covering the coalfields and be invited to initiate a programme for their revision. (Para 79)

   iii. The Board should extend the priorities for investigating likely subsidence damage and consequent preventive work to include sensitive community areas such as residential neighbourhoods. (Para 80)

   iv. Accurate prediction of the effects of subsidence on all drainage systems should be available before mining begins as a basis for discussion of preventive and remedial measures. (Para 81)

   v. The Board should issue further guidance to its Areas on the way in which subsidence costs should be incorporated in the appraisal of mining proposals. (Para 82)

   vi. Coal should not normally be extracted where the Board predicts that severe or very severe damage is likely to occur unless action can be taken to reduce the likelihood of damage below this level. (Para 83)

   vii. The Environment Departments, in revising Class XX (Class XVII in Scotland) of the General Development Orders, should explore ways of achieving tighter control over new underground development. (Para 85)

187. *Modifications to Mine Design*

   viii. Further research should be undertaken into the possible reduction of subsidence by the underground stowage of colliery spoil. (Para 87)

   ix. The Board should encourage the wider application of experience drawn from the success of some experiments with modified mine design in reducing surface damage. (Para 88)

188. *Preventive and Precautionary Works*

   x. Public discussion of the scope for preventive and precautionary measures for domestic, as well as other properties, should follow the wider notification of the approach of mining which we recommend. (Para 90)

xi. The cost of precautionary measures required by the planning authority should be shared between the developer and the Board on a basis to be settled between them. (Para 94)

xii. Government Departments should be prepared to adjust the various capital expenditure allocations made to local authorities to take account of additional expenditure incurred as a result of serious damage to an area. (Para 95)

xiii. The Board should not be liable for compensation for any re-siting or deferment of development which is required by local authorities acting on the improved information about mining intentions available to them. (Para 96)

Notification and Publicity

189. *Local Authorities and Major Developers*
   i. The Board should have a statutory obligation to make available its five year colliery plans to mineral planning authorities (equivalent in Scotland) and to up-date them annually. (Para 102)

   ii. A "notice of approach" should be issued to County and District Councils (equivalent in Scotland) at least twelve months before a coal face becomes operational. (Para 102)

   iii. When so requested by local interests, the Board should establish Technical Liaison Committees through which to interpret their up-dated plans and to elaborate the information they provide. (Para 103)

   iv. Copies of the Board's five year plans should be available for public inspection in local authority offices throughout mining areas. (Para 104)

190. *Householders*
   v. In addition to the publication and display of annual press notices, the Board should be required to notify individual householders usually within two or three months of undermining. (Paras 106 and 109)

   vi. The precise method of notification should be related to the particular circumstances of the area likely to be affected by mining and should be settled in consultation with the District Council. (Paras 107 and 109)

   vii. The Board should consider giving also a broad indication of the likely severity of damage in the light of experience with the new procedures for individual notification. (Para 108)

191. *Mining Enquiries*
   viii. The Government should bring the Law Society and the Board together to agree a form of mining search to be used by those advising prospective purchasers of property in mining areas. (Para 110)

ix. The Board should be required to register each settled claim for compensation with the District Council: the authority would thus be able to disclose to a prospective purchaser that there had been a claim, leaving the purchaser to make further enquiries of the Board. (Para 111)

x. This provision (para 111) would be without prejudice to present arrangements whereby prospective purchasers commission detailed mining reports from the Board in return for an appropriate fee. (Para 112)

The Repair of Subsidence Damage

192. *Repairs or Compensation?*
   i. Future legislation on subsidence should confirm the Board's primary duty to repair damage and to make payment in lieu only in exceptional circumstances. (Para 114)

   ii. There should be no limit of time for claims for subsidence damage compensation. The onus of proof of the cause of damage should switch to the claimant after three years from the date when the damage should reasonably have become apparent. (Para 115)

   iii. The Board should have a clear liability to restore property damaged by mining subsidence to its pre-damaged condition so far as this is practicable. (Para 116)

193. *Repairing Subsidence Damage*
   iv. Claimants should have a right to choose whether subsidence damage should be repaired by the Board or whether an agreed payment should be made to contractors to enable the claimant to repair the property. (Para 117)

   v. The amount of any payment to meet the cost of repairs should be based on an agreed schedule of work, the proper completion of which would be the subject of a final inspection. Reference to independent adjudication should be available in case of dispute. (Para 118).

   vi. Responsibility for supervising repair work and certifying its proper completion should rest on claimants or their representatives when they elect to repair their own property; these responsibilities should rest on a named agent employed by, or acting for, the Board when the latter undertake the work. The Board should consider employing professional advisers as managing agents if their own resources become too thinly spread. (Para 119)

   vii. Repair contracts commissioned by the Board should provide for final inspection in accordance with normal commercial practice; satisfactory completion should be certified by a qualified surveyor who is independent of the Board and counter-signed by the claimant or their representative. (Para 120)

viii. Where "term contracts" are negotiated by the Board with material suppliers, separate contracts against agreed schedules should be drawn up for individual properties and managed up to final inspection as for any other contract. (Para 121)

ix. The Board should require claimants to accept payment in lieu of repairs only in special circumstances. Independent adjudication should be available in case of dispute. (Para 122)

x. A decision by the Board to demolish, rather than repair, a property should be subject to conditions concerning price, the re-housing of the claimant and the care of the site; independent adjudication should be available in the event of dispute. (Para 123)

194. *Interim Repairs*
xi. The use of 'stop notices' should be available to the Board whenever further ground movement is expected, but new conditions governing their use and renewal are required — including proper review procedures. (Para 124)

195. *Temporary Accommodation*
xii. The siting and standard of temporary accommodation, the facilities it provides, and the likely period of occupation should be settled in consultation with a claimant who has to leave his home; local authority housing officers should be asked to assist in the event of dispute. (Para 126)

xiii. The Board should take responsibility for the care and supervision of property temporarily vacated at their request. (Para 127)

196. *Assistance to Claimants*
xiv. The Board should contribute towards the fees incurred by claimants needing specialist advice regardless of the size of the claim. (Para 128)

xv. The scale of fees paid to advisers should be reviewed; payments made by the Board in respect of claimants' advice should be sent to claimants who, as clients, would settle with their advisers: a code regulating the conduct of advisers would not be practicable. (Paras 129 and 130)

197. *Land and Public Utilities*
xvi. The Board should issue guidance to its Areas stressing that the restoration of agricultural land affected by subsidence is the normal practice: payments in lieu should be made only in exceptional circumstances and after full and early consultation with the Ministry of Agriculture, Fisheries and Food (DAFS or WOAD in Scotland and Wales respectively). (Para 132)

xvii. The Board should issue similar guidance on the restoration of drainage systems affected by subsidence: legislation should be revised to make clear the Board's prime duty to put damage right. (Para 133)

Scope of Compensation Provision

198. *Incidental Costs*
   i. The Board should have a statutory obligation to meet reasonable expenditure incurred in the proper pursuit of admitted claims now dealt with under the Code of Practice; independent adjudication should be available in case of dispute. (Para 138)

199. *Stress and Strain*
   ii. Special provision for compensation to individuals who suffer distress arising from subsidence damage would not be practicable; the Board should concentrate on removing the cause by improving the operation of their procedures for restitution. (Para 139)

200. *Inconvenience and Disturbance*
   iii. A payment for loss of home amenity should be available to householders who suffer inconvenience and disturbance related to the duration and severity of damage; this should be incorporated into a new Code of Practice. (Paras 140 to 142)

201. *Loss of Property Values*
   iv. Statutory provision should be made for the payment of compensation for residual loss of property value arising from structural distortion and this should be extended to include clearly identifiable material and physical change in the condition of a property. (Paras 146 and 147)

   v. Publicity should be given in the new Code of Practice to the criteria which govern the Board's decision whether to purchase property; independent adjudication should be available in case of dispute about the decision to purchase or the financial settlement. (Para 149)

   vi. The Board should initiate discussions with the building societies without delay on a possible provision to meet difficulties in granting mortgages for property in mining areas. (Para 150)

202. *Consequential Loss*
   vii. No new provision for compensation to commercial and industrial undertakings for loss of profits or reduction of trade following subsidence damage is called for; the Board should make special efforts to assist small enterprises to maintain their activity and consider hardship payments in exceptional cases. (Para 153)

   viii. Compensation should be available, based on loss in value, for the effects of long term damage on the overall efficiency of an entire agricultural holding. (Para 154)

   ix. A commuted sum, to discharge the Board's liability, should be paid by the Board to public authorities to meet any increased maintenance and running costs following repairs to equipment where this is agreed between the parties. (Para 156)

Resolving Disputes

203. *Existing Provisions*

   i. The Board and the Department of Energy should ensure that relevant booklets, leaflets and forms include information about claimants' right to appeal against Board decision on subsidence compensation; letters rejecting claims should similarly refer to claimants' right to independent adjudication. (Para 159)

204. *A New Appeal Body?*

   ii. The Lands Tribunals are the most appropriate bodies to consider appeals on mining subsidence damage; an entirely new appellate body would not be justified at the present time. The Tribunal's procedures should be examined, and three years after the new arrangements come into effect their membership and practices reviewed. (Paras 160 to 162)

   iii. There is a place for local independent adjudication by persons who have appropriate skills and are drawn from an approved list. The Department of Energy should invite nominations for such a list of adjudicators to be available throughout coal mining areas. (Paras 163 and 164)

   iv. Reference of a dispute to independent adjudication should be by agreement between a claimant and the Board; the consent of the latter should not be unreasonably withheld. (Para 163)

   v. A dispute should be referred from the independent adjudicator to the Lands Tribunal only when the adjudicator considers it the more appropriate body to hear the appeal or when the Board or the claimant wish to appeal on a point of law. (Para 163)

205. *Contributions to Claimants' Costs*

   vi. The award of costs by the Lands Tribunals should normally follow the event as for other appellants. The Board should, however, consider adopting a practice followed in some other areas of dispute in seeking only a nominal sum from an unsuccessful small claimant acting in person when the Tribunal considers that the claimant has not acted unreasonably in bringing the appeal. (Paras 165 to 167)

   vii. Where disputes are referred to independent adjudication, the parties should meet their own costs. The fees of the adjudicator should be met by the Board. (Para 168)

The Framework of Control, Management and Monitoring

206. *The Framework of Control*

   i. The 1957 and 1975 Acts should be consolidated and extended to ensure greater consistency and clarity of scope and intent. The heads of claim in the present Code of Practice should be brought into statute. A new Code should be drawn up by the Board covering a wider range of discretionary payments. (Para 170)

207. *A Separate Commission?*
  ii. The transfer of responsibility for administering the compensation scheme from the Board to a new Commission would not achieve the benefits which can be expected from improvements to the existing arrangements. (Paras 174 and 175)

208. *Management Practice*
  iii. The Board should prepare a public statement in general terms in which their policies on compensation for subsidence damage are made clear. (Para 177)

  iv. Guidance to Areas on the implementation of the Board's compensation policy should include a revised Code of Practice and a procedures manual. (Para 178)

  v. The performance of the Areas in dealing with compensation claims should be monitored by a management audit review team independent of Area management, and reporting to a Board Member. (Para 179)

  vi. The Board should be required to report annually to the Secretary of State for Energy on their administration of the compensation scheme, and their report should be made public and laid before Parliament. (Para 180)

209. *Management Information and Staff Resources*
  vii. The Board should carry out systematic analyses of trends in subsidence claims and costs. (Para 181)

  viii. The Board should review the information needed at Headquarters and in the Areas to secure control over expenditure and to monitor performance effectively. (Para 181)

  ix. The Board should introduce more flexibility in the deployment of staff to meet changes which occur in the workload in the Areas; they should be more willing to employ outside specialists to supplement their own resources. (Para 182)

ACKNOWLEDGEMENTS

Our enquiry could not have been made unless a great many people had been willing to help us.

We have referred in the introductory chapter to the local press and radio stations that told those living in coal mining areas about our work, and prompted the letters and discussions which became a valuable part of the evidence we received. We record in Annex F the names of the authorities, Members of Parliament, professional consultants and corporate bodies who submitted written evidence, and those who in addition attended one of our meetings and patiently answered our questions. We are indebted to them all.

From the outset, we have made continuing demands on the National Coal Board, both at Headquarters and in the Areas. The Board's officers have arranged for the many visits which it seemed useful for us to make; they have done their utmost to find the information we needed, whether from records already available, or brought together to meet our particular requirements. Immediate responsibility for our relationship with the Board has been in the hands of Mr Alan Dickie, the Board's Director of Estates, who acted as one of the two Technical Assessors to the Committee. He has attended all our meetings save those at which evidence was received; his ability to make us aware of the Board's view of the problems we discussed, whilst accepting the independence of the Committee and its duty to reach its own conclusions, has earned our admiration and respect.

We have had the help of Mr Peter Spurrier, Chief Mining Engineer to the South Yorkshire County Council, who was appointed as our second Technical Assessor by the local authority associations. He, too, has attended all our meetings save those concerned with the taking of evidence. We have been dependent on his advice in seeking information from local authorities; where necessary, he has sought and analysed for us comments on particular issues from all local authorities in mining areas. Throughout we have been greatly helped by his wide knowledge and experience of mining subsidence and the working of the compensation scheme. His contribution to our work has proved invaluable.

The importance we attached to direct discussions in mining areas with more than one hundred and fifty of those affected by mining subsidence added greatly to the work which would in any event have fallen on our Joint Secretaries, Mr Richard Greenwood of the Department of Energy, and Mr Richard Footitt of the Department of the Environment. Detailed arrangements for these visits and for our other meetings, and much correspondence, has been in the hands of Miss Elizabeth Ruszka of the latter Department, who served throughout our work, and of others in both Departments who helped for varying periods especially during our visits and discussions in the mining areas. Mr Greenwood and Mr Footitt have analysed with clarity and judgement the large volume of material we received, and faithfully expressed the views that developed amongst us. We are grateful for their devotion to the task and for the wisdom and good humour with which it was discharged.

GLOSSARY OF TERMS

Adjudication : Determination of disputes either by reference to the Lands Tribunal, or to the less formal intervention of a suitably qualified independent adjudicator.

Agent : Professional (eg surveyor) employed by a claimant to act on his behalf in the pursuit of a claim.

Angle of Draw : The angle between the edge of the coal working and the outer limit of ground movement on the surface caused by subsidence.

Arbitration : Method of resolving disputes as currently available in the Code of Practice, as distinct from formal Arbitration generally applied under the Arbitration Acts 1950, 1975 and 1979.

Backstowing : The action of totally or partially filling up the void left underground by mining activity with waste material or specially quarried material.

Code of Practice : The voluntary agreement made by the Board in 1976 to extend their liabilities.

Damage Notice : The form completed by a claimant notifying the Board that he has witnessed damage to his property or land which he thinks is attributable to coal mining subsidence.

Deep Mining : Mining in which access to the coal seams is obtained by means of vertical shafts or inclined roadways driven from the surface and where the coal is extracted by underground working.

Face : Place where the coal is being won from the seam.

General Development Order : Statutory instrument giving deemed planning permission for certain types of development.

Longwall Mining : The method of mining in which coal is cut or otherwise extracted from a straight face or wall of coal, so that the face advances for several hundred metres in parallel strips.

Managing Agent : Professional employed by the Board to manage settlement of a claim.

Panel : The area of coal to be worked by a single coal face which, seen from above, is often rectangular in shape and may be up to 250 metres in width and 1000 metres in length.

Precautionary Measures	:	Measures incorporated in the design of new building development in an area subject to future mining in order to minimise subsidence damage.
Preventive Measures	:	Measures taken on an existing building in an area subject to future mining to minimise subsidence damage.
Remedial Measures	:	Repairs carried out to damaged property.
Stop Notice	:	Notice issued by the Board informing that emergency repairs only will be carried out because further damage is expected to occur within a specified period. Such a notice may be issued under Section 3 of the Coal Mining (Subsidence) Act 1957.
Working Facilities Orders	:	An Order granted by the High Court under the Mines (Working Facilities and Support) Act, giving the Board the necessary facilities to work coal where the Board did not have existing rights to work and were unable to negotiate such rights.

ANNEX B

TECHNICAL ASPECTS OF SUBSIDENCE

The Occurrence of Subsidence

1.   Some degree of subsidence is an unavoidable effect of modern deep coal mining operations and occurs wherever such mining takes place. Virtually all coal mining in Britain is now by the longwall method in which a panel of designed dimensions is extracted from a seam. Typically the seam may be about 1.5 metres thick and the panel up to 250 metres wide and 1000 metres long. As its name implies a wall of coal is continuously cut across the width of the panel and each cut results in the progress of the face further into the coal seam. The rate of this progress is, typically, about 25 metres a week.

2.   The panel may be either cut directly from an access road as shown in Figure 1, which is known as the advance method, or two roadways may first be driven down each side of the panel and the face started at the far end, as shown in Figure 2. This is known as the retreat method and because it allows the geology of the seam to be known before the main extraction takes place and gives better working conditions, it is being increasingly used.

3.   In modern mining no attempt is made to support the strata overlying the worked out part of the panel, apart from the narrow strip of working area immediately behind the face and for advance mining alongside the roadways, and it is allowed to collapse progressively into the void as the coal face advances. The collapse is transmitted to the surface by the successive lowering of the overlying strata within a zone of influence as shown in Figure 3.

4.   The angle between the outside edge of the zone and the vertical is known as the angle of draw, and is typically about 35° for coal measures strata in Britain. As can be seen from Figure 3, as the depth of a given extract increases so the surface area influenced increases, although this is compensated for by a decrease in the vertical settlement at the surface.

5.   A given point on the surface may be considered as being supported by a cone of underlying strata, as shown in Figure 4. The significance of this is that any extraction within the cone will contribute to the surface lowering at that point. Furthermore the greater the depth to the seam, the greater the area supporting a given point on the surface, and the longer that point will be affected as workings progress through the cone. Normally subsidence is more or less contemporaneous with working and thus normally starts soon after the face enters the cone of support and ceases after the face has passed through, although time dependent processes can sometimes mean that the surface effects do not occur until after mining has passed.

6.   The maximum vertical settlement at a point on the surface due to mining from a given seam, which rarely exceeds ninety per cent of the thickness

71

extracted, will only take place if the whole of the seam within the cone is removed. In Figure 4 this is represented by the distance AB for the shallow seam or CD for the deep seam and is known as the "critical width". Extraction of less than this width will result in less than the maximum possible subsidence at the surface, as shown in Figure 5a, whilst extraction of a greater width, known as a super-critical width, will result in a section of the surface experiencing maximum subsidence, giving a flat bottomed, dish shape cross-section as shown in Figure 5c.

7. Figure 5 also shows the levels of strain at different points of the cross-section for the various types of workings. It is apparent from these diagrams that subsidence can leave a property located on the side slopes of a subsidence depression in a permanent state of tilt and in either permanent tension or compression. The surface in the flat section of a subsidence depression resulting from a super-critical extraction (Figure 5c) is not left in any permanent state of tilt or strain, although it will have undergone the maximum vertical lowering.

Damage to Property

8. It is not, however, the vertical lowering per se which causes damage to property, apart from where absolute levels are important as in drainage systems, but the passing of the subsidence wave. This is illustrated in Figure 6 which shows how a property is affected as the coal face advances. As in Figure 5 there are points of extension and compression and it is these strains which cause the damage to property. Generally speaking the shallower and the thicker the seam extracted the sharper the subsidence wave and the more damaging it will be. The rate of advance is another factor, with higher rates giving less time for structures to accommodate movement and damage more likely to occur. Other factors which can exacerbate the effects of subsidence are latent weaknesses resulting from previous (and often unrecorded) workings in the intervening strata, which are activated by and aggravate the new movement, and faulting, which tends to concentrate relative movement at the interface between the faulted strata. This can result in very severe damage to properties situated across the fault line.

9. Voids from previous workings are of particular concern where they are very shallow, that is less than about five times the thickness of the seam extracted, because they can collapse through to the surface. These voids were left by old "pillar and stall" workings in which pillars of coal were left in place to support the roof. For deeper workings the weight of the overlying strata usually crushed the remnant pillars but for shallower workings the voids can remain open for decades or even centuries, although their collapse can be hastened by ground movements induced by modern mining.

10. For a given surface movement, damage to a structure depends on its shape, orientation, design and construction. Structures which are either not strong enough or not flexible enough to withstand or accommodate the strains imposed will suffer damage and the larger a structure the greater the differential strain it will experience. Large buildings, spans or arches therefore tend to be more vulnerable to ground movement. Various measures, known as precautionary measures, can be incorporated during

72

construction to minimise damage from subsidence such as the CLASP system based on a special flexible framework, or the use of "raft" foundations which are placed on a bed of granular material allowing them to slide and accommodate a certain amount of ground movement. Measures can also be taken to reduce damage to existing buildings such as trenching around the foundations to absorb compressive movements or the cutting of "slots" in buildings to reduce the effective size of the structure. These are known as preventive measures.

11.   Where damage does occur it can vary from slight cracks in plaster, sticking doors and windows to the extreme of severe fractures, and buckling of roofs and walls. Indeed, the Board have evolved a classification of damage to property, reproduced in the table below.

TABLE 1   CLASSES OF SUBSIDENCE DAMAGE

Class of damage	Description of typical damage
1 Very Slight or Negligible	Hair cracks in plaster. Perhaps isolated slight fracture in building, not visible on outside.
2 Slight	Several slight fractures showing inside the building. Doors and windows may stick slightly. Repairs to decoration probably necessary.
3 Appreciable	Slight fractures showing on outside of building (or one main fracture). Doors and windows sticking, service pipes may fracture.
4 Severe	Service pipes disrupted. Open fracture requiring rebonding and allowing weather into the structure. Window and door frames distorted. Floors sloping noticeably, walls leaning or bulging noticeably. Some loss of bearing in beams. If compressive damage, overlapping of roof joints and lifting of brickwork with open horizontal fractures.
5 Very Severe	As above but worse and requiring partial or complete rebuilding. Roof and floor beams lose bearing and walls lean badly and need shoring up. Windows broken with distortion. Severe slopes of floors. If compressive damage severe buckling and bulging of the roofs and walls.

Underground Services

12.   All underground services can be damaged as a result of the strains set up during subsidence although the larger, more rigid structures tend to be more vulnerable, particularly sewerage systems, which are also affected by changes in gradient. In particular, sewers can suffer both fractures and pulled joints, leading to the escape of foul water or the inflow of groundwater. Reduction in the designed gradients of sewers can reduce flow rates and lead to silting whilst the reversal of gradients will result in backflooding. In some cases such problems may not become apparent for perhaps several years after the initial damage has occurred.

13.   Precautionary measures may be taken to reduce possible damage from future mining such as the design of sewerage systems with sufficient capacity and gradient to overcome any adverse effects of subsidence and, as with other pipeline systems, the use of flexible joints. Where permanent changes in levels have occurred, however, relaying of sewers with pumping from a collection

point may also be necessary. Preventive measures may be appropriate for some underground services as, for example, with high pressure gas pipelines where the surrounding soil can be removed thereby allowing the pipeline to accommodate any ground movement.

Land Drainage and Waterways

14.   Land drainage can be considered as a hierarchy of systems, both natural and man made, which transport water to its normal destination — the sea. It includes perforated or porous pipe drains laid to improve agricultural land which does not drain naturally, ditches or natural watercourses, intermediate drainage channels, and main rivers. The water authorities have a statutory responsibility for the general supervision of land drainage and direct responsibility for main rivers. Internal Drainage Districts, specified under statute, are administered by a Board with powers to maintain and improve the local drainage system whilst responsibility for the maintenance of small watercourses lies with the riparian owner or occupier, although the local authority can make improvements under the Land Drainage Acts. Canals, which are primarily for navigation but which also may play a part in water resources management, are the responsibility of the British Waterways Board.

15.   All of these systems may be affected by subsidence, usually from changes in levels rather than physical damage, and it is for this reason that flat, low lying areas tend to be more vulnerable. The pipe drains in field drainage systems are fairly robust and do not normally suffer damage themselves although changes to relative levels can upset drainage patterns, sometimes requiring the pipes to be relaid. More generally, if parts of a field are lowered to the level of the water table, ponding can occur leading to a permanent loss of land. On a larger scale, lowering of land in some areas can increase the risk of more general flooding and require the construction of special embankments and pumping stations.

16.   Rivers, canals and watercourses can also be affected by changes in levels, often requiring regrading or new embankments to ensure river flow or to avoid flooding. Weirs may need to be raised to maintain upstream river depths whilst increased gradients can lead to erosion from faster river flows. New river levels may also require modificiations to bridges, to maintain headroom, and to jetties and outfalls.

17.   In general remedial measures should be designed in response to a long term and global view of the effects of subsidence on a given river system. Furthermore, many problems of a more temporary nature can be avoided if mining advances, as far as is possible, in the opposite direction to river flows thereby avoiding the creation of negative gradients.

Mining Techniques to Minimise Subsidence

18.   Several mining techniques are available to minimise the degree of subsidence although they inevitably have an associated cost and may give rise to other problems. One very effective method, however, quite often used by the Board is partial extraction where unworked coal is left between panels

74

and panel widths are reduced below critical values. This is illustrated by Figure 7, which also shows how workings progress over time and how they may be limited by an underground fault. Typically about 50% of available coal may be extracted, and sometimes up to 70%, with relatively little surface subsidence.

19.   Alternatively a complete pillar of coal may be left in place under particularly sensitive installations or buildings of exceptional architectural or historic significance. This may complicate access to adjacent coal however, and will also result in a subsidence "shoulder" on the surface around the sterilised area. In addition there is obviously the net value of the coal left in place to consider and compensation may be required to be paid to the Board for coal sterilised under the Mining Code.

20.   Another technique is "harmonic mining" in which panels are worked in such a way that their subsidence effects tend to cancel each other out. This, however, requires the working of one panel to be closely related to the working of another, a difficult constraint in an area where economic viability is heavily dependent on the rate of working and where the progress of a given panel can be held up by unforeseen problems.

21.   Depending on the depth of working and the compression from overlying strata subsidence can also be reduced by up to 50% with backstowage, that is using the waste material extracted to help fill the void created. However there are many associated problems which would need to be overcome before backstowage could be used with British mining methods. These problems include the need to support and make safe the area being packed, the extra costs, particularly of returning the waste from the separation plant located on the surface and the extra noise, dust and water involved. Backstowage is nevertheless used in some circumstances in other countries and further research to overcome these problems may make it practicable and justifiable in particular cases in Britain.

Figure 1

SINGLE LONGWALL PANEL (Advance)

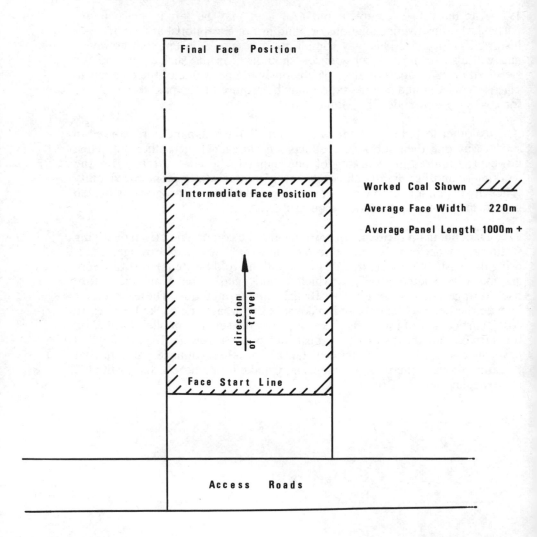

Final Face Position

Intermediate Face Position

direction of travel

Face Start Line

Access Roads

Worked Coal Shown ////

Average Face Width   220m

Average Panel Length 1000m +

Source : South Yorkshire MCC

SINGLE LONGWALL PANEL (Retreat)

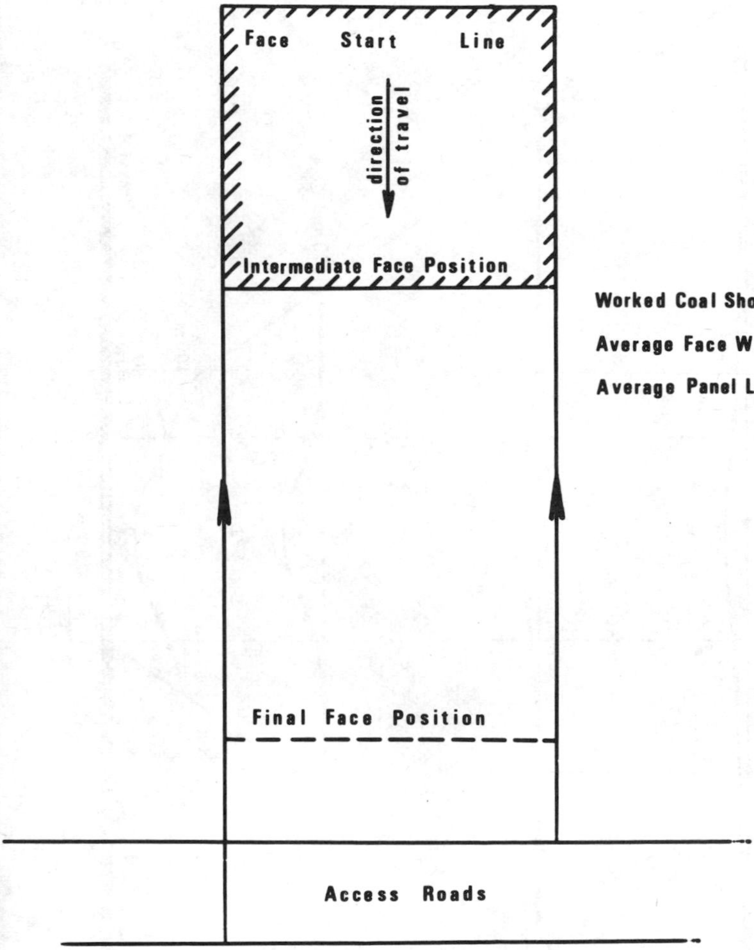

Face Start Line

direction of travel

Intermediate Face Position

Worked Coal Shown /////

Average Face Width   220m

Average Panel Length 1000m +

Final Face Position

Access Roads

Source : South Yorkshire MCC

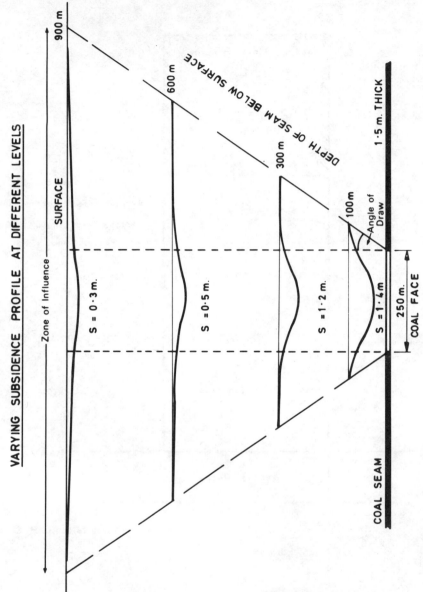

Figure 3

VARYING SUBSIDENCE PROFILE AT DIFFERENT LEVELS

Source: NCB

INFLUENCE OF DEPTH ON TIME (SECTION)

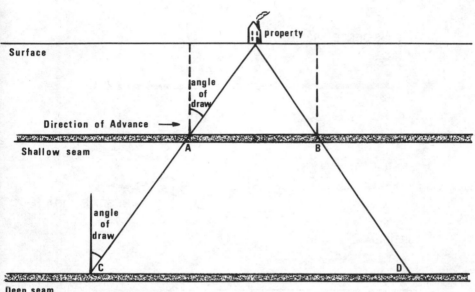

Source : South Yorkshire MCC

79

Figure 5

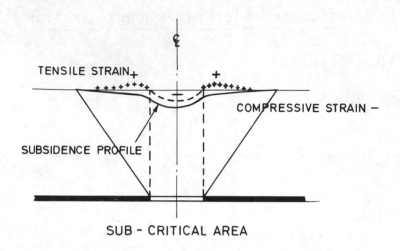

SUB - CRITICAL AREA

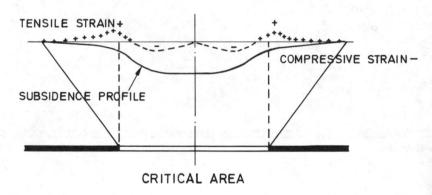

CRITICAL AREA

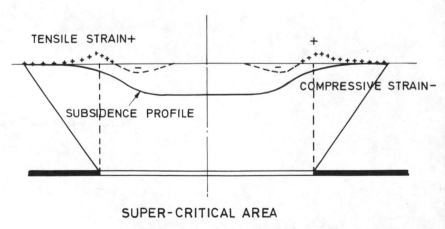

SUPER-CRITICAL AREA

Source: NCB

DEVELOPMENT OF SUBSIDENCE

(not to scale)

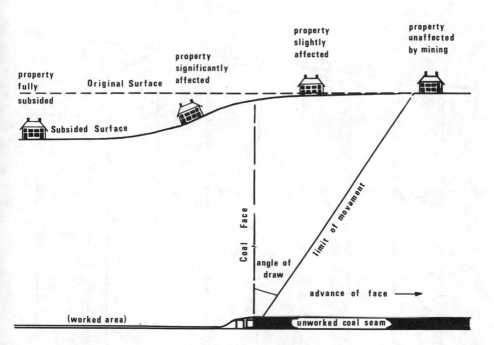

Source : South Yorkshire MCC

81

Figure 7

PATTERN OF MULTIPLE LONGWALL FACES
AND PILLARS

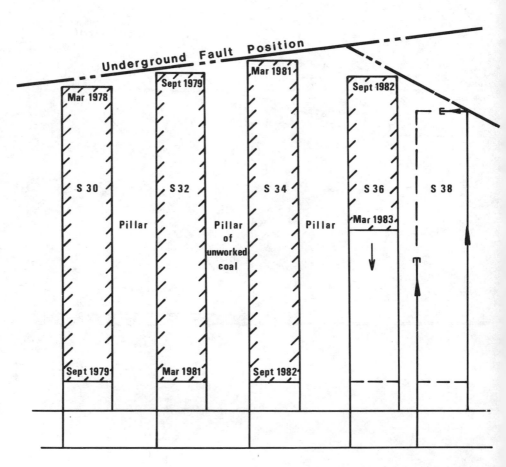

Underground Fault Position

Mar 1981

Sept 1979

Mar 1978

Sept 1982

S 30

S 32

Pillar

S 34

Pillar
of
unworked
coal

Pillar

S 36

Mar 1983

S 38

Sept 1979

Mar 1981

Sept 1982

Worked Coal Shown ⁄⁄⁄⁄

Source : South Yorkshire MCC

82

ANNEX C

FLOW CHART FOR THE PROGRESS OF A CLAIM FOR A DOMESTIC PROPERTY

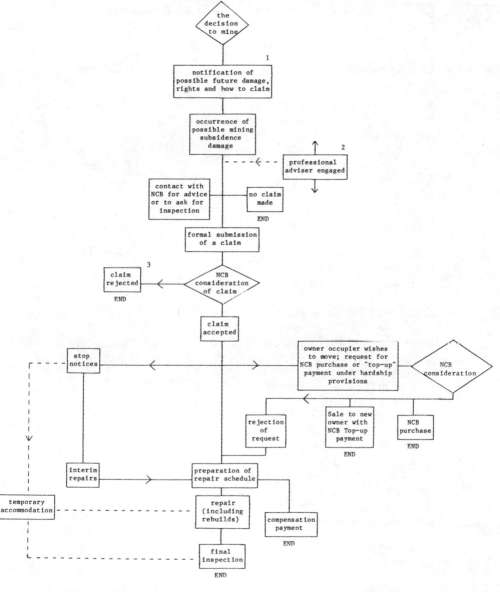

otes

1. Under the Coal Industry Act 1975, as explained in Chapter 2, notice of subsidence is deemed to have been given where the Board had a previous right to work coal. Notification is not therefore generally given at present (although it is recommended that it should be — see Chapter 5).

2. A claimant may decide to engage a professional adviser at any stage.

3. Once a claim has been submitted to the Board disputes between the two parties may arise in the various areas, beginning with the question of liability for damage. We describe the appeal procedures available in Chapter 2, but the point to note here is that an appeal may result in a reversal of a decision of the Board.

LIST OF AREAS VISITED BY COMMITTEE MEMBERS

Groups of Committee Members visited the following localities and called on people, selected at random, whose homes had been damaged by mining subsidence.

Locality visited	NCB Area
Knottingley (Yorkshire)	North Yorkshire
Pontefract (West Yorkshire)	,, ,,
Rothwell (West Yorkshire)	,, ,,
Darton (South Yorkshire)	Barnsley
Staincross (South Yorkshire)	,,
Elsecar (South Yorkshire)	,,
Hoyland (South Yorkshire)	,,
South Kirkby (South Yorkshire)	,,
Carr Vale (Derbyshire)	North Derbyshire
Inkersall (Derbyshire)	,, ,,
Middlecroft (Derbyshire)	,, ,,
Mansfield (Nottinghamshire)	North Nottinghamshire
Kirkby-in-Ashfield (Nottinghamshire)	South Nottinghamshire
Cotgrave (Nottinghamshire)	,, ,,
Hucknall (Nottinghamshire)	,, ,,
Calverton (Nottinghamshire)	,, ,,
Barlaston (Staffordshire)	Western Area
Upper Longdon (Staffordshire)	,, ,,
Silverdale (Staffordshire)	,, ,,
Tunstall (Staffordshire)	,, ,,
Coalville (Leicestershire)	South Midlands
Bagworth (Leicestershire)	,, ,,
Donisthorpe (Leicestershire)	,, ,,
Eskbank (Lothian)	Scotland
Saline (Fife)	,,
Clydach Vale	South Wales
Ynysybwl	,, ,,
Hopkinstown (Pontypridd)	,, ,,
Oakdale	,, ,,
Crumlin	,, ,,
Berthillwyd (Treforest)	,, ,,

ANALYSIS OF EVIDENCE FROM THE PUBLIC

NCB AREA	TOTAL NUMBER OF LETTERS	1	2	3	4	5	6	7	8	9	10	11	12	13	14
SCOTLAND	2	1	1	-	-	-	-	-	-	-	-	-	-	-	-
NORTH EAST	16	5	4	6	-	1	8	-	6	5	-	1	1	1	2
NORTH YORKSHIRE	51	15	14	12	13	2	25	2	-	22	4	-	3	3	-
BARNSLEY	100	26	29	25	9	14	41	28	16	61	7	6	8	7	1
SOUTH YORKSHIRE/DONCASTER	25	5	5	9	-	3	8	-	4	10	-	1	1	3	4
NORTH DERBYSHIRE	6	3	1	1	-	2	5	-	2	3	-	-	2	-	-
NORTH NOTTINGHAMSHIRE	40	14	9	16	10	9	9	-	8	13	-	3	3	-	-
SOUTH NOTTINGHAMSHIRE	48	17	9	13	6	16	18	7	4	22	2	-	5	2	1
SOUTH MIDLANDS	19	7	9	7	-	2	9	6	-	12	-	-	4	2	1
WESTERN	75	21	10	20	16	10	22	6	9	21	11	15	2	10	-
SOUTH WALES	46	5	17	16	-	4	9	-	-	13	3	3	11	2	2
TOTAL GB	428	119	108	125	54	63	154	49	49	182	27	29	40	30	11

KEY TO HEADINGS

1 = Dissatisfaction over contact with the Board (complaints about the attitude of officers, difficulty in contacting officers, the length of time taken to deal with enquiries etc).

2 = Recurrence of damage (frequently with denial of liability by the Board).

(contd.)

85

3 = Rejected claims (reasons given by the Board including: last workings being too old to have caused damage, compensation already paid to previous owners, damage resulting from dilapidation, particularly for older property, or no reason being given at all).

4 = Lack of information from the Board, for example, on the possibility of damage occurring, how to claim, the claimant's rights.

5 = Dissatisfaction with the advice given to claimants by professional advisers.

6 = Dissatisfaction with repairs (the standard of work, attitude of the contractors, length of time taken to complete the work).

7 = Dissatisfaction with temporary accommodation (complaints about the length of time claimants were away from their own homes and the standard of the temporary accommodation).

8 = Complaints about lack of compensation for consequential loss (financial losses suffered through damage to furniture and fittings, loss of earnings, expenditure on repairs which was not compensated by the Board).

9 = Stress, strain and illness caused by the damage itself, disturbance during repairs or difficulty in gaining full restitution.

10 = Loss of property value.

11 = Difficulty or suspected difficulty in selling damaged properties.

12 = Lack of follow-up by the Board.

13 = Cases where properties were demolished or purchased by the Board.

14 = Compensation payments (dissatisfaction with the amount, lack of knowledge of what the amount covered).

These 14 headings were identified as being the main areas of concern for the householders who presented written evidence. In studying the anlaysis, it should be remembered that householders were given no guidelines on the content of their submissions - the issues raised were entirely those of most concern to them. Inevitably the table can not give any indication of the weight given to particular issues by those writing in, but merely records the number of times an issue was raised. The majority of letters dealt with more than one issue.

In some instances it proved difficult to identify the NCB Area responsible for an individual postal address. This was due mainly to the fact that some localities were the responsibility of two NCB Areas, and explains why the analyses for Doncaster and South Yorkshire Areas have been combined.

86

ORGANISATIONS AND MEMBERS OF PARLIAMENT WHO SUBMITTED EVIDENCE

Those marked * gave oral evidence in addition to written evidence

Local Authority, Governmental, Nationalised Industry and Professional Bodies

Association of Drainage Authorities*
Association of County Councils*
Association of District Councils*
Association of Metropolitan Authorities*
Barnsley Law Society*
Barnsley Metropolitan Borough Council*
Borough of Blaenau Gwent
Borough of Newcastle-under-Lyme
British Gas
British Property Federation*
British Railways Board
British Waterways Board*
Building Societies Association*
Citizens Advice Bureau
City of Stoke-on-Trent*
City of Wakefield Metropolitan District Council*
County Planning Officers Society*
Country Landowners Association
Electricity Supply Industry
Fife Regional Council*
Forestry Commission
Institution of Geologists*
Institution of Municipal Engineers
Islwyn Borough Council
The Law Society*
Leicestershire Branch of the Association of District Councils
Longdon Parish Council
Lothian Regional Council*
Melton Borough Council*
Ministry of Agriculture, Fisheries & Food
National Association of Local Councils*
National Farmers Union*
Nature Conservancy Council
Northumberland Association of Local Councils
Nottinghamshire County Council*
Over Whiteacre Parish Council
Renfrew District Council
Royal Institution of Chartered Surveyors*
Royal Town Planning Institute (Scottish Branch)

Scottish Society of Directors of Planning
Scottish Landowners Federation
Selby District Council*
Severn-Trent Water Authority
South Yorkshire County Council*
Teesdale District Council*
University of Leeds
Welsh Water Authority
West Bretton Parish Council
West Glamorgan County Council*
West Yorkshire Metropolitan County Council*
Yorkshire and Humberside County Councils Association*
Yorkshire Water Authority

Other Bodies

J M Bellis (Chartered Surveyors)
Blackwood Hall Farms Ltd
Blackwood Pig Farms Ltd
Booth & Coupe (Mining Subsidence Surveyors)
Alan Brentnall (Surveyors, Auctioneers, Estate Agents and Valuers — Mining Subsidence Claim Consultants)*
Charbonnages de France
CRACK — Committee of Residents against Coalmining under Kinoulten
Darton Subsidence Action Group*
Eyre Brothers (Barnsley) Ltd
Fennell, Green & Bates (Chartered Surveyors)
Heath & Cantlay (Solicitors)*
Hinchliffe's (Chartered Surveyors)*
Holmes, Ralph & Sons (Dairy Farmers)
Hoyland & District Property Owners Association*
Michael P Jubb and Co. (Mining Subsidence Surveyors)
Kent, Jones and Done (Solicitors) (Mr A A Reeves*)
Millers Lane Action Group
Nottingham Area of the National Union of Mineworkers
Nationwide Building Society
Property World (Mr John Sankey) (Estate Agents, Valuers, Surveyors)
Roberts Mining Surveyors & Subsidence Consultants
Round (Consulting Mining Engineers)*
Ruhrkohle A G
John Sankey (Estate Agents)*
Gordon Shaw and Associates (Chartered Architects and Surveyors)
Sherwood Forest Golf Club Ltd
South Kirkby & Moorthorpe and Hemsworth South District Electoral Wards of the Labour Party
George Yarwood FRIBA (Chartered Architect)
Yorkshire Naturalists' Trust Ltd

Members of Parliament

The Rt Hon Jack Ashley CH MP	Stoke on Trent South
The Hon Adam Butler MP	Bosworth
John Heddle Esq MP*	Mid-Staffordshire
Geoffrey Lofthouse Esq MP*	Pontefract and Castleford
Allen McKay Esq MP	Barnsley West and Penistone
The Rt Hon Roy Mason MP	Barnsley Central
Alec Woodall Esq MP*	Hemsworth

Additional Institutions and Individuals giving Evidence

Professor Atkinson, Department of Mining Engineering, University of Nottingham

J R Bridgford and Sons (Chartered Surveyors)

British Geological Survey

Carver-Smith, Garnett and Associates, Chartered Architects, Chartered Town Planners (Mr G W Garnett)

Gwilym Roberts Esq, Formerly MP for Cannock and Burntwood

Professor C T Shaw, Professor of Mining Engineering, Imperial College of Science and Technology, University of London

North Yorkshire County Council

The Rt Hon Eric Varley, Formerly MP for Chesterfield

Wardell Armstrong (Consulting Mining Engineers)

THE INDEPENDENT SURVEY OF PUBLIC ATTITUDES TOWARDS THE PRESENT COMPENSATION SYSTEM

1. The objective of the survey was to obtain an independent assessment of peoples' attitudes to the present compensation system and to find out if there was a significant "take-up" problem by those entitled to claim. The survey was therefore designed to cover a number of relatively small areas where it was known that there had been a higher than average incidence and severity of damage in order to yield a high number of people whose houses had suffered subsidence damage and who could relate their experiences. The survey was carried out by Research Services Limited, who were appointed after competitive tendering in July 1983.

2. In all ten such areas were selected to ensure that a good cross-section of circumstances would be covered, including different types, tenures and ages of housing, different mining patterns, and including some areas where "stop notices" had been used. Since the operation of the present compensation system was being examined, it was important to select areas that had been affected since 1976, when the Code of Practice was introduced. Furthermore, only residential areas were sampled since other sectors, such as industry or agriculture, had their own organisations to present their views to the Committee in addition to the evidence we received directly. In the interests of economy, the areas selected were confined to Yorkshire and the Midlands; but the NCB Areas in which these areas are situated account for the great majority of claims.

3. A total target of 1000 interviews with people whose homes had suffered damage was set and allocated between the ten sample areas to broadly reflect the importance of the corresponding NCB Areas in terms of their number and cost of claims. The minimum number of interviews set for each area and the actual number of successful interviews carried out, totalling 1079 interviews, is shown in Table 1. The location of the sample areas is shown in Figure 1.

4. After a pilot exercise, interviews were held in the ten areas during the period 10 to 27 August, taking care to avoid local holiday periods. Despite the time of year there was a high contact rate and only about two per cent of those contacted refused to be interviewed, with most people very willing to relate their experiences:

addresses selected for interview	2255
no contact after 2 or more calls	309
potential interviewee sick, temporarily away, etc	52
interview refused	52
contact made for interview	1842
ineligible for interview (no subsidence damage)	763
interview held	1079

5. The questionnaires on which the interviews were based covered all possible aspects of an individual's experience including the following main areas:

   i.   advance notification of possible subsidence and its source (including the Board);

   ii. sources of advice on the cause and extent of possible mining subsidence damage;

   iii. sources of advice on how to make a claim and the use of professional advisers;

   iv. for claims contested by the Board, the reasons given and details on any further action;

   v.   the way in which claims were handled by the Board;

   vi. degree of satisfaction with the way in which repairs were carried out and their quality;

   vii. degree of satisfaction with the payment of compensation, where applicable;

   viii. degree of satisfaction with any temporary accommodation provided by the Board;

   ix. where applicable, details on any "stop notices" that had been issued (time in force etc);

   x.   where applicable, any difficulties over selling a property because of mining subsidence and whether the Board were approached to help with the sale;

   xi. attitudes towards the system as a whole and any suggestions for improvements;

   xii. background information on the property, the subsidence damage and on the occupants.

6. The replies to the questionnaires were collated and expressed in terms of the percentage of a sample who agreed or disagreed with a particular statement or who belonged to a particular category. These percentages have been extensively used in the report to highlight the strengths and weaknesses of the current system. Where such a percentage is based on the total sample, and where it is around fifty per cent, the standard error of the estimate is about 1.5 percentage points. This means that the estimate is likely to be within ± 3 percentage points of the value for the whole area sampled. (Twice the standard error gives the ninety five per cent confidence interval). Any move away from estimates around fifty per cent leads to a slight decline in the standard error and therefore also of the confidence interval. The estimates are of course based on samples from a few selected areas, deliberately chosen to have a high incidence and severity of subsidence damage. The figures therefore do not represent average conditions in mining areas or even typical conditions, but they do relate to the experiences of over 1000 homes and provide an invaluable quantified guide to the problems and issues involved.

Table 1:

Sampling Frame for the Attitude Survey on the Current Compensation System

Area Sampled	NCB Area in which sampled area lies	Target number of interviews	Actual number of interviews
1. Pontefract	North Yorkshire	100	127
2. Pogmoor	Barnsley	150	197
3. Goldthorpe	South Yorkshire	100	107
4. Inkersall	North Derbyshire	75	84
5. Carr Vale	North Derbyshire	75	84
6. Deepdale	North Nottinghamshire	75	86
7. Ravensdale	North Nottinghamshire	75	99
8. Hucknall	South Nottinghamshire	125	135
9. Coalville	South Midlands	50	62
10. Silverdale	Western	75	98
TOTAL		900*	1079

* plus another 100 interviews across the ten areas.

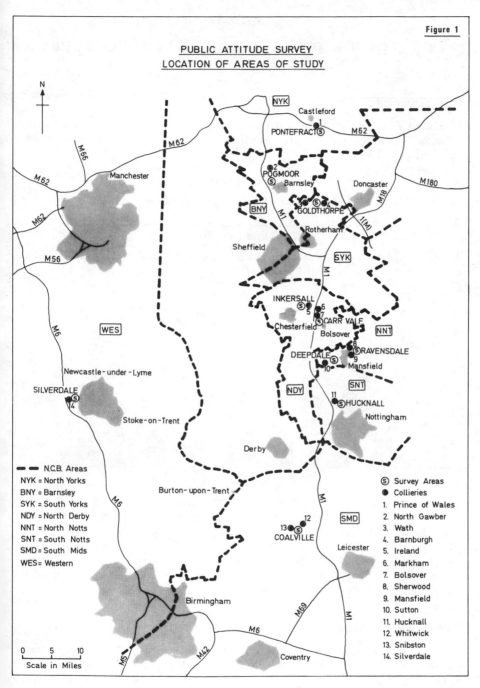

ANNEX H

COSTS OF SUBSIDENCE COMPENSATION AND VERY SEVERE DAMAGE TO DWELLINGS

Costs of Subsidence

1.   Table 1 below shows the costs to the Board of subsidence compensation for admitted claims in both current prices and constant 1974/5 prices since the financial year 1969/70.

Table 1

Subsidence costs for admitted claims

Financial Year	Current Prices	Constant 1974/75 Prices
	£m	£m
1969/70	5.1	9.2
1970/71	5.4	8.7
1971/72	6.3	9.1
1972/73	6.2	8.2
1973/74	7.9	9.6
1974/75	10.1	10.1
1975/76	14.4	11.6
1976/77	17.0	12.1
1977/78	26.0	16.6
1978/79	30.9	17.8
1979/80	42.6	21.3
1980/81	54.7	23.3
1981/82	87.9	36.3
1982/83	89.8	33.8

2.   An analysis of costs by NCB Area for the latest annual figure available (1982/83) is given in Table 2. The total for this year of £89.8 million is rather less than the expenditure for "surface damage" appearing in the "Expenditure on Revenue Account" of the Board's published accounts (£144 million) since the latter includes certain provisions for future expenditure on damage which is not yet the subject of admitted claims and also expenditure related to the restoration of opencast coal sites.

'Very Severe' Damage

3.   Information on the incidence and costs incurred by 'very severe' damage was requested from the Board by the Committee and is reproduced in Table 3. The Board do not normally differentiate between categories of severity of damage in their accounting system and figures were therefore extracted using the following definition of 'very severe' damage:

    i.   where a house or other building has to be demolished OR

    ii. where a house or other building requires substantial rebuilding OR

94

iii. where farmland or other land is made permanently unusable for its normal purpose OR

iv. where damage to a public utility service or works of a statutory undertaker are damaged so as to require emergency action on a substantial scale.

4. It should be noted that the above definition of 'very severe' damage in relation to domestic properties is more restricted than the definition of very severe damage given in Table 1 of Annex B and only includes the most severely affected properties of this category.

5. The Committee also asked the Board to identify those collieries which are principally responsible for any appreciable amount of very severe damage as defined above. The Board provided the following list of collieries two of which, Rothwell and Snibston, have since been closed:

North Yorkshire Area
Prince of Wales
Rothwell
Nostell

Barnsley Area
Woolley

North Derbyshire Area
Markham/Ireland

North Nottinghamshire Area
Sherwood
Mansfield
Sutton

South Midlands Area
Donisthorpe
Rawdon
Snibston

Western Area
Hem Heath
Florence
Lea Hall

Administration

6. The Committee requested information on the administration of the subsidence compensation scheme and although the Board were unable to provide figures on costs, because of the other duties carried out by the departments involved, they were able to give information on the deployment of Estates Department staff, the department primarily responsible for administration of the compensation system. The figures provided by the Board are reproduced in Table 4.

Table 2 — *Subsidence Costs for Admitted Claims by Area, 1982/83 and Number of Claims Admitted in Year Ended 31 August 1983*

SECTOR	SCOTLAND	NORTH EAST	NORTH YORKS	DONCASTER	BARNSLEY	SOUTH YORKS	NORTH DERBY	NORTH NOTTS	SOUTH NOTTS	SOUTH MIDLANDS	WESTERN	SOUTH WALES	TOTAL GREAT BRITAIN
Houses (£m)	0.07	0.50	2.60	0.18	1.50	1.43	11.54	23.10	18.20	0.95	0.96	0.11	61.14
Agricultural (£m)	0.03	0.05	1.00	0.14	0.80	0.33	0.97	0.60	0.42	0.61	1.24	0.02	6.21
Industrial/Commercial (£m)	0.02	0.03	0.40	—	0.90	0.40	0.31	1.20	0.92	0.19	3.37	—	7.74
Statutory Undertakers/ Public Authorities (£m)	0.12	0.13	3.30	1.67	1.20	1.15	1.98	1.30	1.36	0.86	1.58	0.08	14.73
Total All Sectors (£m)	0.24	0.71	7.30	1.99	4.40	3.31	14.80	26.20	20.90	2.61	7.15	0.21	89.82
No. of Claims (All Sectors) Admitted in Year Ended 31 August 1983	91	353	1507	219	2385	1401	4733	7869	3772	453	1431	301	24515

Table 3 — *Incidence and Costs of "Very Severe" Damage by Area 1982/3*

	SCOTLAND	NORTH EAST	NORTH YORKS	DONCASTER	BARNSLEY	SOUTH YORKS	NORTH DERBY	NORTH NOTTS	SOUTH NOTTS	SOUTH MIDLANDS	WESTERN	SOUTH WALES	TOTAL GREAT BRITAIN
NUMBER OF "VERY SEVERE" DAMAGE CLAIMS HOUSES ONLY													
Total Number of House Claims	76	246	1,140	77	2,082	1,592	3,842	5,300	3,243	531	1,145	157	19,431
Cases of "Very Severe" Damage	1	7	51	—	—	—	61	300	19	6	10	—	455
"Very Severe" cases as a percentage of total House claims	1.3%	2.8%	4.5%	—	—	—	1.6%	5.7%	0.6%	1.1%	0.9%	—	2.3%
COSTS OF "VERY SEVERE" DAMAGE CLAIMS													
Houses (£m)	0.02	0.07	0.13	—	—	—	0.99	4.62	0.09	0.20	0.03	—	6.15
Agricultural (£m)	—	—	—	—	—	—	—	0.30	—	—	0.04	—	0.34
Industrial/Commercial (£m)	—	—	0.03	—	—	—	—	0.48	—	0.10	0.03	—	0.64
Statutory Undertakings/Public Authorities (£m)	—	—	0.13	—	0.18	—	—	0.26	—	0.30	0.08	—	0.95
Total All Sectors (£m)	0.02	0.07	0.29	—	0.18	—	0.99	5.66	0.09	0.60	0.18	—	8.08
Saleable Coal Output (Million Tonnes)	6.6	12.4	8.4	6.8	8.1	7.3	8.1	12.4	8.3	8.2	10.8	6.9	104.3
Cost per Tonne for "Very Severe" Damage — (New Pence)	0.3p	0.6p	3.4p	—	2.2p	—	12.2p	45.6p	1.1p	7.3p	1.7p	—	7.7p

Table 4 — *Deployment of Estates Department Staff on Subsidence Compensation by Area*

NUMBER OF ESTATES DEPT STAFF INVOLVED IN WORK ON SUBSIDENCE COMPENSATION		SCOTLAND	NORTH EAST	NORTH YORKS	DONCASTER	BARNSLEY	SOUTH YORKS	NORTH DERBY	NORTH NOTTS	SOUTH NOTTS	SOUTH MIDLANDS	WESTERN	SOUTH WALES	TOTAL GREAT BRITAIN
PART-TIME	Prof/Tech	8	4	3	6	1	2	3	6	2	3	14	2	54
	Admin and clerical	4	2	2	1	1	1	2	—	—	1	6	—	20
	Total	12	6	5	7	2	3	5	6	2	4	20	2	74
FULL-TIME	Prof/Tech	—	8	9	—	15	10	23	12	18	8	17	4	124
	Admin and clerical	—	1	3	—	5	1	8	3	6	1	4	1	33
	Total	—	9	12	—	20	11	31	15	24	9	21	5	157
PART-TIME AND FULL-TIME	Prof/Tech	8	12	12	6	16	12	26	18	20	11	31	6	178
	Admin and clerical	4	3	5	1	6	2	10	3	6	2	10	1	53
	Total	12	15	17	7	22	14	36	21	26	13	41	7	231

Printed in the UK for HMSO
737085.5.84.39180